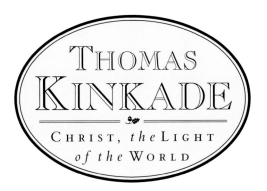

THOMAS
KINKADE

CHRIST, *the* LIGHT
of the WORLD

A DEVOTIONAL

Published in Nashville, Tennessee, by Thomas Nelson, Inc.
Unless otherwise noted, Scripture quotations are from
THE NEW KING JAMES VERSION. Copyright © 1979, 1980, 1982, Thomas
Nelson, Inc., Publishers.

Scripture quotations noted NRSV are from the NEW REVISED
STANDARD VERSION of the Bible. Copyright © 1989 by
the Division of Christian Education of the National Council of The Churches of
Christ in the U.S.A. All rights reserved.

Library of Congress Cataloging-in-Publication Data
Kinkade, Thomas, 1958-
Christ, the light of the world : a devotional / Thomas Kinkade,
with Anne Christian Buchanan and Debra Klingsporn.
p.   cm.
ISBN 0-7852-6961-4
1. Advent Prayer-books and devotions—English.
2. Christmas Prayer-books and devotions—English.
I. Buchanan, Anne Christian. II. Klingsporn, Debra. III. Title
BV40.K55   1999
242'.33—dc21   99-34353
                    CIP

Printed in the United States of America.

1 2 3 4 5 6 – 04 03 02 01 00 99

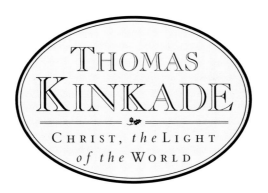

THOMAS
KINKADE

CHRIST, *the* LIGHT
of the WORLD

A DEVOTIONAL

THOMAS KINKADE

with

ANNE CHRISTIAN BUCHANAN

and

DEBRA K. KLINGSPORN

THOMAS NELSON PUBLISHERS
Nashville

DAY 1 | THE SEASON COMES

For the vision is yet for an appointed time;
But at the end it will speak, and it will not lie.
Though it tarries, wait for it;
Because it will surely come.

HABAKKUK 2:3

"You have twenty-four more shopping days until Christmas," says the unwelcome voice on drive-time radio—and the December countdown begins. Twenty-four days of frenetic activities, a rush of preparations, and the frantic fear that "I'll never get it all done." December means shopping, wrapping, decorating, baking, school parties, seasonal concerts, and packages to get in the mail. For many people, the very thought of December invites exhaustion. The dates on the calendar are unyielding, unforgiving, never offering us more of what we think we want and need—more time, more energy, more quiet, more of that elusive feeling we call the "Christmas spirit."

For those who celebrate the coming of Christ, though, December has another dimension. With December comes the weeks of Advent. Yet, the month of December and the season of Advent are not synonymous; they are, in fact, radically different. December brings all the outward preparations, all that we have to do to prepare for Christmas. Advent is an invitation to an inward preparation, calling us to listen, to attend to the preparation of the heart. Advent calls us to stop—however briefly—all of the frenetic doing and invites us to come to into an experience of the holy.

Although not all churches observe the liturgical season of Advent during the four weeks before Christmas, observing Advent in our homes offers a welcome alternative to the frenzy of December's demands. Advent is a season, not an event; a spiritual discipline, not a calendar date. Historically a time of rich tradition and meaningful reflection within the Church, the word *advent* comes from a Latin root that means "coming." Advent is an experience of anticipation, an invitation to prepare for the coming of the light of Christ into our world.

So in the days to come I ask you to sit quietly with the images from my brush and imagination, images that are meant to beckon you into a world of stillness. Allow your heart to wander on a reflective journey through the season of Advent even as you attend to the demands of December. "The journey begins with Advent," wrote author Jan Richardson. "Advent is a dance set to the rhythm of waiting. We wait for the holy, we wait for the birth, we wait for the light . . . Advent reminds us that we are a pregnant people, for God calls each of us to bring forth the Christ."[1]

I invite you to an experience of inner watching and expectant waiting; to listen with your heart; to be attentive to the presence of

God within even the most mundane moments. The coming of Christmas, the season of Advent, invites you to come to a manger and experience anew the wonder, the beauty, the glory of Christmas.

Oh, God, as I close my eyes and allow my mind to go the quiet place I see on this page, help me learn how to welcome Advent and prepare for the coming of Christmas. God, I am so quickly caught up in the busyness of the season as I rush frantically through my daily "to do" list. Bring me into the stillness, into Your presence, that I may learn what it means to "wait on the Lord," to welcome Your coming in this holy season.

DAY 2 | ON TIPTOE

Let the heavens rejoice, and let the earth be glad;
Let the sea roar, and all its fullness;
Let the field be joyful, and all that is in it.
Then all the trees of the woods will rejoice before the Lord.
For He is coming. . .

PSALM 96:11-13

If there is any image that summarizes Christmas for me, it's that of tiny children standing on tiptoe or jumping up and down, breathlessly anticipating the days to come. The month or so before Christmas is a kind of delicious torture for little ones. They're not exactly clear on how long it is until the big day, but they know they just can't wait.

As we grow older, of course, we lose a lot of that eager impatience. We think instead of how much there is to do and how little time is left to get everything done. Eagerness turns to anxiety: "only _____ more shopping days . . ." Waiting on tiptoe turns into trying to survive the season.

That's why I think we need to take a step back (sometimes again and again) to remember what this getting-ready-for-Christmas time, the season traditionally known as Advent, is all about.

Quite simply, it's about waiting with the right attitude. And the right attitude for Advent is a child's attitude: eyes wide open, watching for the wonder.

Remember what Jesus said about little children and the kingdom of heaven? He said we need a child's spirit in order to live in God's kingdom. And surely part of this required childlikeness, especially in the before-Christmas season, is relearning what it means to wait in breathless anticipation.

What specifically are we waiting for?

On the surface, we're waiting for the holiday itself—for the joys of family togetherness, for a day when the daily grind (plus the accelerated grind of the preparations) finally grinds to a halt and celebration takes over. We wait for a day of giving and receiving, of worship and play. That's certainly worth waiting for and planning for.

In a spiritual sense, we wait once more for the coming of Christ. We're reenacting the drama of prophecy and longing and joyous fulfillment that climaxed with Jesus' incarnation. We're reliving all those centuries of waiting in darkness for the great light to shine, as well as those personal eons in our lives when we feel like we too are waiting for the light of Christ to shine in us.

In the ancient cycle of the Church calendar, Advent has also been a time when Christians remember that we're still waiting for the final arrival of the kingdom of God in all its fullness. Yes, Christ has come into our world. Yes, the battle between light and darkness has been won. Christmas has happened. Easter has changed everything. But the final chapter has not yet been played out. There's more to come. And we're waiting for that too.

When I remember this, I realize that the Advent message of waiting on tiptoe is even more important. It ties in with the Scriptures that remind us to watch and wait always, because we just don't know when the next events are going to unfold. And it reminds us that this is something to wait for not with fear and dread, but with careful preparation and eager anticipation.

The Scriptures tell us this over and over again: *Wait! There's more. Keep your eyes open. It could happen at any moment!*

Like little children at Christmas, we don't exactly understand the timetable, and that makes some of us a little edgy. But there's nothing really wrong with that. We're not supposed to be blasé or complacent about the coming of Christ—either at Christmas or at the end of the age.

Even as we throw ourselves into all the "to dos" of getting ready for Christmas, all the responsibilities of our daily lives and the extra responsibilities of the season, a part of us needs to be waiting for our Lord with eyes wide open, watching for the big moment.

Waiting to celebrate that His kingdom has come on earth.

Waiting to renew our understanding of His coming in our lives.

Waiting for His final coming again in glory.

Waiting on tiptoe—like a little kid waiting for Christmas.

Dear Lord, in this season of anticipation, renew my sense of wonder and excitement. When the days speed by, help me to slow down enough to open my eyes. Remind me why I'm waiting—and why it's worth waiting for. And remind me always that the waiting is not in vain—that You have come, and that You are coming, and that it's all going to be good.

DAY 3 | TIME FOR DISCOVERY

My soul magnifies the Lord,
And my spirit has rejoiced in God my Savior . . .
For He who is mighty has done great things for me,
And holy is His name.
And His mercy is on those who fear Him
From generation to generation.

LUKE 1:46-50

The girls usually start asking before the Thanksgiving turkey is out of the oven. Patience is not one of their virtues.

"Mom, can we pull out the Christmas stuff?"

"Dad, can we just get out the box with our nutcrackers?"

"Mom, how about just the bag of Christmas stuffed animals?"

"We promise we won't make a mess in the attic. Can't we open just one box and pull out a couple of things?"

In the Kinkade household, traditions run deep and memory is long. The day after Thanksgiving, out come the Christmas CDs and the familiar carols fill the house. The anticipation of pulling out the boxes of decorations is almost as great as the anticipation of Christmas itself—I did say *almost!* The day we pull down the attic stairs, retrieve dusty boxes from eleven months of storage, and begin pulling out tree lights, garlands, decorative Santas, Nativity figures, red bows, and Christmas quilts is a day of discovery. The mystery of Christmas begins again in the simple act of opening a box and seeing something at once familiar and yet new, picking it out of its nesting place—and remembering.

"Oh, Mom, Dad, remember this? Remember how we found it at that little shop in the mountains when Chandler was all polka-dotted from the chicken pox?" Each box, once opened, becomes a family treasure chest, a rediscovery of memories and moments. No matter how many years the same decorations are packed away, we somehow forget what the boxes hold; pulling it all out again awakens something deep within us. Christmas is a time when the past and present merge as they do at no other time of the year. The "hopes and fears of all the years" surprise us in small moments and seemingly insignificant acts. Memory and anticipation intertwine like the garlands and lights we hang.

To pull out dusty boxes of carefully (or sometimes hurriedly) packed decorations is an act of hope, a bold act of faith that says in the very doing that Christmas will come again, that in this home we will proclaim the coming of a Christ child, and that despite whatever limitations we may face in our circumstances, our finances, even our relationships, we again prepare to discover anew the presence of Christ in the world. To open boxes of decorations is to open our hearts. To pull back dusty lids is to pull back the shroud of "ordinary" that blinds us to wonder and mystery and to proclaim that we are once again willing to welcome the coming of Christ into our homes, our hearts, our everyday lives.

Former Yale University chaplain and seminary president John Vannorsdall said, "To set up a tree in the house, to bake special cookies, take time from work, set aside money, to gather in whomever we can of friends and family, to surround ourselves with special music of great power; these things create a radical change in what is ordinary in our lives. It is a magic time."[2]

So pull out the boxes. Discover the treasure chests of memories and moments. And welcome again the magic of Christmas.

God of light and God of darkness, God of memories and moments, help me again discover the wonder that awaits me in the coming of these days. Fill my heart with gratitude for each day, each month, each year of life I've been given. As I pull out lights and stockings, garlands and ornaments, let me again be thankful for all the living each represents. And as I move from room to room, I pray that a spirit of gratitude will fill my heart as I fill my home with sights and sounds of Christmas. May my home and my family as well as my spirit continue to magnify You . . . through the season and all through our lives.

DAY 4 | MAKING ROOM

For unto us a Child is born,
Unto us a Son is given;
And the government will be upon His shoulder.
His name will be called Wonderful, Counselor, Mighty God,
Everlasting Father, Prince of Peace.

ISAIAH 9:6

I've been through it four times now—the exciting, exhausting process of getting a house ready for a new baby. There's so much to think about! So much to do!

With our first child, we didn't really know what we were doing. We read books and talked with our mothers and collected advice. We scouted garage sales for the equipment we would need. We were nervous and elated and a little frightened, all at the same time.

With each successive baby, we've become a little more confident, but there are still a lot of questions. Who's going to sleep where now? Should we buy a new crib or move the little one into her toddler bed? What do we need, and what do we already have? Is the house still baby-proofed? Do we remember what to do? How do we prepare the older girls for the little one who is coming?

And in the midst of it, even the fourth time around, there is that wonderful sense of anticipation. Who is this new little one going to be? Will she be like her sisters? What will we name her? When exactly will she get here? Will she even be a she? (In our case, all four times, the answer was yes!)

In a way, I think, getting ready for Christmas is like that time of getting ready for a baby. In reality, it *is* getting ready for a baby. There is a lot to do—and we will enjoy His coming far more if we take the time to make preparations.

For a baby, the preparations are partly external—the crib, the car seat—and partly internal—adjusting our minds and hearts to welcome someone new into the family.

For the celebration of the coming of Christ, that's true as well.

During this time of joyful anticipation, we prepare the externals of our lives for the celebration—cleaning the house, decorating our homes and offices and towns, buying new clothes or putting on special clothes we love to wear each season, setting out the things that remind us of Christmas. (Come to think of it, the malls have been exhorting us to prepare the externals for several months now.)

But even more, we would do well to prepare ourselves on the inside.

"Let every heart prepare Him room," the carol says.

That's what I think we all should be doing during these weeks before Christmas—preparing the rooms of our hearts for the coming of Christ.

How do we do it?

By cleaning out our inner lives, deliberately putting away the resentments and the distractions that clutter our hearts and minds, and by giving a priority to forgiveness and reconciliation in this season of relationships.

By rearranging our obligations to make sure there's room for prayer and reflection in the midst of all the busyness.

By decorating our hearts with thoughts and attitudes that are worthy to welcome a king—love and joy and peace—and by decorating our lives with loving deeds.

Most of all, by setting aside the time and the space for inner preparation—time to read and listen, time to pray, time to ponder. Time to reflect on what it means that the One whose name is Wonderful Counselor, Mighty God, Prince of Peace . . . still came in the form of a tiny, vulnerable human child.

Let every heart prepare Him room.

Heavenly Father, I cry with the psalmist: "Create in me a clean heart." I want to be ready whenever You come. As I clean my home and begin to get it ready for the big day, show me how to prepare my heart as well. After all, that's the place where You live. 🍃

DAY 5 | TRANSFORMATION TAKES TIME

*But we all . . . are being transformed
into the same image from glory to glory,
just as by the Spirit of the Lord.*
2 CORINTHIANS 3:18

The wreath says it all. Red bow, perfectly tied; placed in just the right spot; gently lit. A welcoming symbol of merriment to come. A circle of festivity. This is the home we all want to come home to—and this is the fantasy few of us actually do come home to. We can imagine what's inside where the warm glow lights the night: Beautiful tree. A fire in the fireplace. Candles burning invitingly. Time to sit quietly, savor the moment, and sip hot cider.

Yet once we pull out the boxes from the attic, most of us confront a time-intensive task with more "task" than "time." We want the transformation of our houses to be completed virtually overnight and are frustrated at how long it inevitably takes. Some homeowners now hire professional decorators to provide a made-to-order transformation. We want a whirlwind of activity, a deco-rating blitz that results in a home ready-made for the season—*now*. We want perfection, but what we have are tangled lights, tired bod-ies, and frayed tempers. We want immediate transformation. But in preparing our home for Christmas—just as in preparing our hearts—immediacy is not necessarily our ally.

As a painter, I spend my days dipping a brush into paint because I love to create beautiful worlds where light dances and peace reigns. But the transformation that turns a blank, white can-vas into a compelling work of detail, light, and wistful romance is one that takes time and patience. Over the years, I've learned that the process is as important as the result.

We all are artists when it comes to preparing the canvas of our homes for the Christmas celebration—and the best gift we can give ourselves early in the season is the recognition that any significant transformation takes time. Each step in the process can be an opportunity to invite God's transforming presence into our hearts and our homes. As we untangle lights, we can pray, "God, bring the light of Christ into this moment." As we arrange green-ery, we can give thanks for the gift of life, for all that grows and gives beauty to our surroundings. As we hang stockings, we can say a silent prayer for each person for whom the stocking is hung. Even the mess of scattered boxes, strewn packing paper, and those Christmas decorations we no longer want to use but can't quite throw away can serve as reminders of a life that is full, blessed, and shaped by love. Rather than working frenetically without pausing to catch our breath, instead pause, remember, give thanks, and most important, enjoy the process.

Lasley F. Gober, author of *The Christmas Lover's Handbook*, says that Christmas "gives us an excuse to be creative, expressive, extravagant, and excessive . . . [We are] moved by the spirit to transform [our] homes into veritable wonderlands of greenery, glimmer, gaiety, and warmth. Come December, pull out all your options and all of your imagination—but not all your energy."

Encourage all members of your family to participate. Get their input on what they want to do the same, what they'd like to change. And remember, memories are made in the doing, not in attaining an ideal.

God of lavish love and transforming grace, open my eyes to the possibilities of beauty before me—even when the "canvas" isn't finished yet. Grant me the patience to enjoy the process of transformation—even the transformations You are making in me. 🌿

DAY 6 | WHAT DO YOU EXPECT?

Therefore the Lord Himself will give you a sign:
Behold, the virgin shall conceive and bear a Son,
and shall call His name Immanuel.

ISAIAH 7:14

The time leading up to Christmas is a time of great expectations. But let's face it, we don't always get what we expect!

I'll never forget the Christmas that my little brother, Pat, asked for one of the year's most coveted toys—a "Johnny Astro" rocket ship. Both of us boys spent the entire month of December in an agony of expectation regarding that anticipated Christmas prize. The TV ads showed a wonderful remote-controlled rocket ship that you could guide around your house at ceiling level. All month we pictured the fun we would have with such a fabulous toy.

Then Christmas morning arrived. Pat unwrapped his Johnny Astro, and what a letdown! What we found in the box was a deflated balloon, some cardboard accoutrements to make the balloon look like a spaceship (though when inflated it just looked like a space blimp), and a little fan to push the balloon around the room. There was no real remote control. You could blow the ship across the room with the fan, but then you had to run over and fetch it. It wouldn't even stay in the air by itself!

I think most of us can recall times like that—a time when the wonderful Christmas we hoped for just didn't turn out the way we planned. Sometimes our expectations just weren't realistic. Sometimes another person let us down—or we failed to live up to our own expectations. Sometimes it rains on Christmas. Sometimes it fails to snow.

Whatever the cause, disappointed expectations can really put a damper on the Christmas season.

Does that mean we shouldn't have any expectations for Christmas? Not at all. The trick, I think, is knowing what to expect—and this becomes a little easier when we realize that the entire Christmas story is full of thwarted expectations!

Surely Mary and Joseph didn't expect to have their first baby in a stable. They weren't expecting a pregnancy in the first place, not to mention a virgin birth! Surely the shepherds weren't expecting their night's work to end with an angel concert, and the Magi didn't envision sneaking out of the country after they brought their gifts.

For Jesus' fellow Jews, His coming as Messiah certainly ran counter to expectation. They were looking for a political revolutionary, someone to get the hated burden of Rome off their back. What they got was a Nazarene carpenter who dined with tax collectors and called their own leaders hypocrites. No wonder they wanted Him crucified! He had disappointed their expectations in a big way.

And what does all this say about Christmas expectations?

Simply this: You can't always expect all your plans to work out—but that doesn't have to spoil your joy. You can't expect all your wishes to be granted—but you might end up with more than you ever dreamed of.

Because you live in a fallen world, in fact, you can more or less expect that things will go wrong—at Christmas as at other times of the year.

And yet we serve a God who is in the business of setting things right. That's the whole point of Christmas.

So here's what I think we should expect from the season to come.

We can expect that God will keep His promises—though not necessarily in the way we have in mind. That's where faith comes in.

We can expect to be surprised—so a little flexibility helps.

Best of all, if we keep our eyes and hearts open, we really can expect to meet Christ in the unfolding of the Advent and Christmas season. Not necessarily as we expected . . . but as He is.

It's right there in the name, after all: *Immanuel.*

It means "God with us."

That's what we can always expect at Advent . . . and what we get.

Dearest Lord Jesus, You are Immanuel, with me in both my joys and my disappointments. You offer me healing for my hurts. You give me good things beyond anything I can ask or expect. Open my eyes to see what You are doing in my life—this season and always. And thank You for Your love, which always exceeds expectations. 🌿

Day 7 | Tending the Inner Fire

Listen to me in silence.
Isaiah 41:1 (NRSV)

To believe that silence is possible in a home with four daughters is to believe in miracles. Although my paintings are serene, my home is not. Squeals of laughter, inevitable disputes of "property" rights, giggles on the phone, stuffed animals flying through the air, or my wife "reminding" them that it's time for piano lessons—our home buzzes with more activity than a beehive in spring. And we love it.

We love hearing little feet padding down the hall in the early morning hours, a snuggly little girl with tousled hair, rubbing her eyes, clutching her blanket and bear, ready to reconnect with Mommy and Daddy after early morning light has interrupted her dreams. We love the sounds of laughter erupting. We love the stampede of girls rushing in from playing outside when called for supper, the blast through the back door, the commotion of all four talking at once. We love the pleading requests for "just one more kiss, Daddy," or "Mommy, that hug didn't count; I need one more," as we tuck one in for the fourth time. And we love the magic time when bedtime brings a contented quiet as sleep descends, activity stills, and the house is silent, but full of all that is most precious to us.

Silence. That magical, mystical moment when we can hear our own thoughts. A time when activity ceases and we can experience the quiet of a household at rest. Christmas without music would be like our house without our girls; but Christmas without silence would be like a day without bedtime. One is as essential as the other. One is incomplete without the other.

Our culture is one filled with noise. The chatter on radios. The rapidly changing images on television. The ringing of telephones. The interruptions of planes overhead. Silence may be golden, but as a culture we are conditioned to avoid it, to fill all waking moments with some kind of noise.

Author and theologian Henri Nouwen wrote, "As soon as we are alone without people to talk with, books to read, TV to watch, or phone calls to make, an inner chaos opens up in us. This chaos can be so disturbing and so confusing that we can hardly wait to get busy again . . . In this chatty society, silence has become a very fearful thing. For most people, silence creates itchiness and nervousness. Many experience silence not as full and rich, but as empty and hollow . . . [Yet] silence is the discipline by which the inner fire of God is tended and kept alive."[3]

We can hear our children breathe only when we are quiet and

close enough to listen. We can hear God whisper only when we intentionally seek moments of silence. To prepare our homes is not enough. Christmas will come and go, and we will sigh with unsatisfied longing if all our preparations focus on what we think needs to be done. To prepare Him room is to make time to enter the stillness, to embrace the quiet, to listen for that "still, small voice."

God, I ask that You quiet the noise in my life, both that which bombards me and that which comes from within. Teach me how to embrace the silence I so often avoid by hurrying to do the next thing. Teach me, O God, to tend the inner fire.

Thomas
Kinkade

DAY 8 | WHAT DO YOU REMEMBER?

Tell your children about it,
Let your children tell their children,
And their children another generation.

JOEL 1:3

Memories—they're the very heart of Christmas. And if you don't believe me, just think about your childhood. Think about your teen years, your young adulthood, the time when your children were small—whichever applies best to you. How many of your most powerful memories are connected with the Christmas season?

Remember all those years you spent the holidays at Grandma's house . . . or the year your family rebelled and resolved to have Christmas at home? Remember the year you asked for a bike and got a puppy . . . or asked for a horse and got a guitar . . . or even the year that Santa didn't come? Remember the joyful year the first baby arrived . . . the bittersweet holiday you spent alone and away from your family . . . the heaviness of the year your mother was sick . . . the emptiness of the year your father died?

The specifics will vary, of course. But chances are, your memory vaults are full of images from Christmases past, because there's something about the Advent and Christmas season that seems to magnify experiences and highlight them in our minds. The happy moments shine like burnished gems. The painful moments stand out in sharp relief. Even the ordinary moments seem to glow. And when you look back on your life, the memories of Christmases past seem to string out behind you like a row of lighted lampposts.

For better or worse, the season of Advent and Christmas forms milestones in our lives. We mark the years with our Christmas memories.

I believe this is exactly as it should be-for remembering, after all, is the whole point of this season. At Advent we remember—by reading Scripture and singing songs and acting out tales—our collective and personal memory of what God has done for us.

We remember what it was like to be human before Christ came . . . what it would still be like if Christmas had not happened. Remember how we walked in darkness, how despite God's best efforts we persisted in straying like lost sheep from His laws and His love?

We remember what the prophets said, what God promised— about a branch growing from the root of Jesse, about lions lying down with lambs . . . about a Messiah who would be misunderstood and persecuted but who in the end would change everything.

Then we remember how it all came to pass . . . with informational angels, with a custom-designed star, with a frightened but obedient young wife and her perplexed but obedient husband-to-be, with a simple baby lying in a pile of straw.

Most of all, we recall the purpose of it all.

He did it for us, remember? He did it to send light into our darkness, to save us from our sins, to give us hope in the midst of a hopeless human condition. And He did it by sending His own Son to take on our flesh and His own Spirit to live in ours.

That is the memory we must hold fast to, whatever other holiday memories crowd our hearts and souls. This is the vital remembrance we must instill in our children and pass along to those who come after us.

After all, as any psychologist will tell you, all memories have the power to shape us. But only these God-given memories—and the reality they invoke—have the power to save us.

And that's a crucial thing to remember . . . year after year after shining year.

Father, in this remembering season, teach me to be thankful for my memories. Show me how to find joy in the good ones, to learn from the difficult ones. And, remind me again and again of the reason this season is really worth remembering: "For God so loved the world that He gave His only begotten Son."

DAY 9 | LOOKING LIKE CHRISTMAS

For the earth shall be full of the knowledge of the LORD.

ISAIAH 11:9

It's beginning to look a lot like Christmas" goes the old Bing Crosby tune. And so it is.

The signs begin appearing early. Some folks say they appear in the stores earlier every year; almost before Halloween has come and gone, we see the telltale evidence of the season to come.

As familiar as pencils and spiral notebooks in August or hearts and cupids in February, if the weather doesn't tell us Christmas is coming, something else does: spools of red ribbon, boxes of Christmas lights, Santa hats and fuzzy red stockings neatly lining store seasonal displays.

Among some Christians, grumbling about the commercialism of Christmas is as common as grumbling about traffic in New York or smog in Los Angeles. To some, garlands that appear overnight in shopping malls, lighted displays in downtown office buildings, and toy catalogs in early November are signs of the misplaced emphasis for the celebration of Christ's birth.

I see it differently.

As an artist, I've learned that what I see is as important as what I do. The image that emerges on canvas is one born of seeing details in light and shadow, perspective of line and dimension, subtlety of color and hue. For an artist, what the eye sees directs what the paintbrush captures. The same is true in our spiritual life: what our eyes see shapes what our hearts feel. We can look and see only the obvious, or we can look and see the hiddenness of God at work in our homes, our lives, our world.

My wife, Nanette, can look about her each day and see only the clutter of four children, or she can see in the clutter the joy, fullness, and gift of four little girls who grace our lives. I can go into my studio and see paints and canvas and chemicals, or I can see raw materials that become part of the mystery of God as I seek His direction in my work. The good news of the gospel has always been given "to those with eyes that see."

"There is no event so commonplace but that God is present within it, always hidden, always leaving you room to recognize him or not to recognize him," wrote author and theologian Frederick Buechner.

For those who have eyes to see, no matter whether the motivation is inspired by commercial gain or not, the end result is the same—the ordinary is cast off, the world around us is transformed, and for a brief time in the darkest days of winter, "the earth shall be full of the knowledge of the Lord."

We can look around us each day and see the obvious, or we can look and see what Albert Schweitzer called the "ineffable mystery" of a God who seeks, a God who comes, a God who reveals Himself.

And so with a grateful heart, I welcome the red bows, the lights, and the store displays in the same way I welcome the hiddenness of God at work in every aspect of my life.

O God, as Albert Schweitzer said so many years ago, "You come as One unknown to those who knew You not." Reveal yourself to me, O Lord, in the lights and in the crowds, in the obvious and in the hidden. Open my eyes that I may see, really see. Come, Lord Jesus, come.

Thomas Kinkade

DAY 10 | OH, TASTE!

Oh, taste and see that the LORD is good;
Blessed is the man who trusts in Him!
PSALM 34:8

I

f I close my eyes right now,
I can almost taste them—the wonderful, delectable flavors
of Christmas.

I think of peppermint. And chocolate. And creamy eggnog . . .
and tangy cranberry sauce. And of course I think of Nanette's wonderful specialty—warm, spicy gingerbread, dusted with powdered
sugar and cut into squares for us and for our guests. The very
thought of it sets my tongue to tingling. The very idea makes me
eager for Christmas to come.

Christmas is, after all, a celebration of the senses, and the sense
of taste usually gets a full workout during the month before the day
arrives. Party tables groan. Homemade goodies show up on desks
and doorsteps. Gourmet catalogs tempt the tastebuds.

No wonder people worry about their waistlines during the Advent season. The plain truth is that Christmas tastes great!

And yes, all this bounty of delicious delight can be a bit of a problem. Food shouldn't be the focus of the season, especially during the "waiting" weeks of Advent. Excess of indulgence doesn't lead to joy, and our banqueting can be hollow if we let ourselves be blinded to the needs of those who might not even get a taste of Christmas.

And yet I believe we need to resist the guilt that tells us that celebrating the wonderful tastes of Christmas is somehow unspiritual or inappropriate. Instead, I believe we need to savor the special flavor of Christmas with a spirit of thanksgiving and joy.

For aren't we getting ready to celebrate the fact that God, a spirit, chose to take on human flesh—including the life of the senses? Including taste?

Remember, we're celebrating the coming of a God who would later take the trouble to turn water into excellent and delicious wine—so good that wedding guests wondered why it wasn't served earlier. We're celebrating a God who spent much of His time on earth enjoying good food with friends, neighbors, even tax collectors and sinners . . . a God who after His resurrection revealed Himself to His followers over a charbroiled fish breakfast and in "the breaking of the bread." We're celebrating a God who has invited us all to a great final banquet at the end of the age—as well as a God who invented our tastebuds in the first place!

And here's something else about the sense of taste that heightens my sense of appreciation for the special flavors of Christmas. Taste, after all, is the most intimate and personal of the senses. To taste something fully, you have to actually bring in into your mouth, to make it part of you. You can't hold something at arm's length and still taste it. And you can't be sure that your experience of a particular flavor will be like anyone else's.

There's something about the sense of taste that gets our attention and inspires our enthusiasm. And I believe God uses that. He invites us to "taste and see that He is good"—to experience His love and savor it in the same intimate way that we enjoy a piece of fudge or a holiday eggnog.

And that's what I think we need to remember as we maneuver our way through the taste-tempting weeks prior to Christmas.

Think of all the wonderful flavors as reminders of just how good God is, how much He loves us.

Think of your tastebuds as daily reminders of how we are to experience our Lord's love—with joy, with a shiver of delight, with a prayer of gratitude, and with the clear understanding that the joys of this Christmas are nothing but a foretaste of joys to come.

Lord Jesus, in this season of pondering and remembering and experiencing, grant that everything my senses encounter will help me connect with the reality of who You are and what You have done for me. More than I crave peppermint or even chocolate, I crave the sweet taste of Your love. Thank You for sustaining me and giving me joy. 🌿

Thomas Kinkade

DAY II | THE SIGNATURE FRAGRANCE

For we are to God the fragrance of Christ among those who are being saved and among those who are perishing.

2 CORINTHIANS 2:15

Have you ever noticed that the sense of smell works like a shortcut to your emotions?

One sniff of something familiar—a perfume, a blossom on a bush, a particular brand of disinfectant—has the immediate power to make you feel happy or sad or fearful or loved. And one sniff is surely all it takes to plunge you immediately into Christmas!

What aromas do that for you? The piney fragrance of wreaths and Christmas trees? The tang of wood smoke in the air? The candle-smell of warm paraffin or the Christmassy bouquet of potpourri? One woman told me the plastic smell of dolls in a toy store is all it takes to make her feel like a child at Christmas!

For me, though, the quintessential Christmas aroma is surely the smell of baking. To walk in the house and breathe in the warm, yeasty fragrance of rising bread . . . the crispy brown-sugar cookie smell . . . the zing of ginger and allspice—that's almost an automatic shortcut to a sense of well-being, of happy anticipation. (In this I'm fortunate to have married a woman who loves to bake!) The fragrance of baking tells me in powerful emotional shorthand that someone is home, that someone cares, that all will be well. The aromas of yeast and fruit and spices leave their mark on the atmosphere of a house that is as distinctive to me as a signature—a signature fragrance of love.

In Jesus' day, too, aromas carried powerful emotional significance. And that was exactly the point of two of the gifts that the Magi brought to commemorate Jesus' birth. The gifts of frankincense and myrrh, in fact, were actually gifts of evocative fragrance.

For many of us, who have never actually smelled frankincense and myrrh, the emotional impact of these gifts has been lost. But from the story itself we can gather a sense of just what they meant. They exuded the aroma of something costly, something beautiful, something sacrificial. In addition, like many of our Christmas memories, they evoked feelings both joyful and bittersweet, for these very fragrances were ones used to prepare bodies for death.

I suspect their essence was similar to the expensive oil of spikenard that Jesus' friend Mary would pour out years later on His feet. The Scriptures say that fragrance "filled the house," the same way the perfume of Nanette's baking wafts through our own household. Jesus Himself clearly understood—and told His disciples—that the fragrance was really the signature of Mary's love.

Surely this was part of what the apostle Paul had in mind when he wrote that we, Jesus' followers, are supposed to be the fragrance of Christ in the world. We are to live in such a way that the lovely aroma of His love floats through the air around us, attracting others by its evocative power.

Now, that's an interesting thought for this Christmas season! Can you imagine your life being as irresistible to others as the smell of bread baking . . . of Christmas trees . . . of candles and dolls and all those other Christmas smells? Can you imagine the fragrance of your life writing a signature of God's love in your own home, in your workplace, in your world?

It's something worth thinking about as you go about your pre-Christmas business. This Advent season, in the midst of all your preparations, don't forget to breathe deeply. Sniff for the scent of frankincense and myrrh so you can recognize the signature of God's love in your life.

And then think how you could live today so that God's signature fragrance of divine eternal love wafts gently and irresistibly toward everyone you meet.

Dear Father, amid all the intoxicating smells of this season, remind me that love is the sweetest scent of all—and it is both costly and precious. Write Your signature on my heart, so that others may breathe in the scent of Your love in my life.

Thomas
Kinkade

DAY 12 | A CRAZY, HOLY GRACE

To seek God, and, it might be, touch and find him; though indeed he is not far from each one of us, for in him we live and move, in him we exist.

ACTS 17:27-28

The decorative Santa stands about two feet tall. He holds a pencil in one hand and a list in the other and, of course, on the list are names of boys and girls. His arms move as though he's writing, adding more names to the list with his pencil—and my girls love to take that pencil! Every year when the Santa comes out of storage, we replace the pencil in his hand, knowing it's only a matter of time before the pencil disappears again.

The girls want to touch that Santa; they want to take hold of that pencil in the same way they want to take hold of the season, as if capturing Christmas is like playing the game "Capture the Flag." Hold a toddler up to a Christmas tree adorned with lights and ornaments, and the first thing the little one does is reach out—

perhaps tentatively, perhaps with bravado—to touch the object of fascination.

When it comes to Christmas—and faith—we want something tangible and real. We want to reach out and touch the holy, and we want to be touched by the holy.

I find it no surprise that in most of the healing stories in the Gospels, when Jesus heals the blind, the sick, and the lame, He does so by touching them.

Countless times I've watched one of my daughters bump a knee or stub a toe and run to Nanette for comfort. Although I've seen the drama played out time and time again, I always stop and watch the drama unfold: the woman I love, whose gentle touch I can't imagine my world without, stops what she's doing and patiently bends to pick up a hurting child, enfolding her in a mother's embrace while gently asking, "Where does it hurt?" She strokes the little one's hair, makes sure nothing's skinned or broken, dries our daughter's tears, and sends her on her way.

This drama between mother and child, a drama as ordinary as making peanut-butter-and-jelly sandwiches, is a daily reenactment of touching the holy and the holy touching us. In those brief moments between mother and child, both are changed, both have given, both have received.

In celebrating Christmas we celebrate the Incarnation, God breaking into human history. We celebrate a God who reaches across time and eternity to touch our lives with "a crazy, holy grace. Crazy because who could have ever predicted it? . . . And holy because these moments of grace . . . heal and hallow."[4]

To touch is to seek, to explore, to know. From the pencil in the

Santa's hand to a mother's comforting embrace to unwrapping presents under the tree, we want our family's celebration to be one of touch, one of reaching out to each other, one of celebrating "a crazy, holy grace."

Redeeming God who reaches across time and eternity, break into my world in this Advent season and touch me with Your crazy, holy grace. In all that I touch today, let me be mindful that I am called to be a carrier of Your love. Let my touch be that of kindness; let my heart be filled with compassion.

DAY 13 | OLD SONGS, NEW MEANING

Having eyes, do you not see? And having ears, do you not hear?
And do you not remember?

MARK 8:18

O*come, all ye faithful . . ."*

It's only the second week of Advent, and already I must have
heard that carol a hundred times—or more. Over the loudspeaker
at the grocery store. On the elevator in downtown office buildings.
From the carolers outside the discount store. Over the car radio.

"Joyful and triumphant, O come ye . . ."

I love this old carol. I love all the old carols. We love to sing
them in our home, loudly and enthusiastically, sometimes on pitch.
We play them on our stereo system—the Christmas CDs come out
of storage even before the boxes of decorations come out of the
attic. The majority of my Christmas paintings took shape to the
strains of the great musical works associated with Christmas—from
Handel's *Messiah* to Bing Crosby's rendition of "Silent Night"!

With the "wiring" of America almost complete, we can do almost anything to a musical accompaniment, and carols can play for us any hour of the day. And this, I think, is a good thing. What we listen to again and again becomes a part of us, almost a part of our souls. And what better thing to be a part of our souls than the words and music of these wonderful old songs about Christmas.

"O come ye to Bethlehem."

We love Christmas carols because they're familiar. We love them because almost everyone knows the words (or at least the first verses!), and so they give us common ground. We love them because they're beautiful, and because they are part of our legacy. They're a perfect way to pass along to our children the story of what Christmas means.

"Come, and behold him . . . "

The only problem, as I see it, with the constant play of Christmas carols during this season is that these old familiar songs can become so old and familiar that we almost don't hear them. Instead of musical expressions of faith, they become holiday background music, setting a pleasant stage for all that we hope to accomplish during the holidays. "O Come, All Ye Faithful" shares equal billing with "Rudolf the Red-Nosed Reindeer." We sing them all by rote and hum them without thinking, and we forget to really listen to the message they are proclaiming.

"Born the King of angels . . . "

How do we reach past the familiarity factor to hear the message of the old songs? Some Christians I know follow the old tradition of not playing Christmas carols during the Advent season. I can see some sense in this. Saving Christmas carols for Christmas Day and afterwards might help us remember that they are special and precious. They are to be listened to with open ears and open hearts, not simply treated as part of the atmosphere.

But I'm just not ready for that. When Christmas is in the air, I want Christmas music in the air as well. But this year I do want to take the time to listen, really listen to what the old carols are telling me. Maybe I'll learn some new verses for the songs I can only sing one stanza of. Maybe I'll even learn what happened to Good King Wenceslas after he saw that man gathering winter fuel!

The Scriptures tell us repeatedly that we are to "sing to the Lord a new song." I don't think that means we're supposed to stop singing the old ones. But I do think we're supposed to sing them with full understanding of how fresh and astonishing their message really is. After all, Scripture also tells us the Lord is in the process of making all things new—and surely that applies even to the eternal message of the songs we've heard a million times before.

"O come, let us adore him, Christ the Lord!"

Lord, open my ears to the new song that sings itself in the midst of the old carols. Give me fresh ears to hear the meaning that speaks in what I've heard so many times before. Grant me grace to love the tradition of Christmas, yet hear its message as though it for the first time.

DAY 14 | A TAPESTRY OF TRADITION

And a little child shall lead them.

ISAIAH 11:6

Go ahead. Just try. Try changing one little thing. If you have kids over the age of three and younger than twenty-five, just try to change where you place the stockings or how you arrange the Nativity or where you hang a wreath. If your house is anything like mine, the protests will be loud, vocal, unanimous, and immediate. If a bumper sticker slogan from an anti-litter campaign in Texas were adapted for our household at Christmas, "Don't mess with Texas" would become "Don't mess with Tradition."

Our daughters' memories are a virtual blueprint for our home's interior design at Christmas. From where we place our tree to what cookies my wife bakes to how we hang the stockings, kids latch on to traditions early—and don't want to let go. Ritual, repetition, and tradition matter.

What is it about these simple things that takes hold of our hearts in such a profound way and won't let go? What we use when we bake cookies, whether our tree lights are colored or white, songs played until we think we'll hear them in our sleep, or even where we hang certain things in our house—these are the threads that weave Christmas memories for our children.

My friend Anne Christian Buchanan wrote in a Christmas memory journal, *The Remembering Season,* "Children are amazingly accepting when it comes to choice of traditions. What they love is the tradition itself. And so it was that our family grew into the habit of a Christmas Eve supper of hamburgers after the evening service at church—hamburgers at the only hamburger joint that was open at that hour on Christmas Eve. It was a tradition we guarded zealously."[5]

Traditions, those things we do again and again, year after year, often without giving them much thought, punctuate our preparation and intensify our anticipation. Christmas traditions, like Christmas memories, are lampposts that light our way and mark our path. Like a worshipful heart, they cannot be imposed, but rather must emerge. Traditions and rituals, like sacraments, are those actions that give expression to that for which words will always be inadequate. Traditions tell a story of what is important, what we as families value, and are what over time—over time—shape our souls, transform our hearts, and link our past with the present.

Often we assume we know what our children "expect," what they think is most important about how we celebrate Christmas. But children have a way of surprising us, of remembering and valuing what is seemingly insignificant. In one family the youngest child places the angel on top of the tree before anything else goes on; in another family, the angel goes on last, a crowning, symbolic act saying the tree is complete, ready for festivities to come.

This year, if you want a fresh perspective on the Christmas experience, try asking the people in your lives—especially the children—what's important to them. What do they look forward to? What would Christmas not be Christmas without? What are their favorite holiday foods? If preparing Christmas dinner became a family activity instead of one person doing it all, what would the meal be like?

Not only will some of the answers surprise you, but as the prophet Isaiah said so many years ago, "and a little child shall lead them."

Lord, let me be like a child, surprised. Remove the tarnish, the cynicism, the obligation from my coming and my going, my giving and my receiving in these short days filled with long hours. Whether the child who might lead me again to wonder is my own, or only a chance encounter in my day, let me be open to what I might learn from one wide-eyed and full of wonder. ❧

DAY 15 | GOOD SENSE OR EXTRAVAGANCE?

From his fullness we have all received, grace upon grace.
JOHN 1:16 (NRSV)

C hristmas won't be Christmas
without any presents!" exclaimed Jo in the classic novel *Little
Women* by Louisa May Alcott.

Indeed! For all the attention given to the value of "simplifying"
Christmas celebrations, I, for one, agree with Jo—as does every
child I've ever known. Christmas in times past may not have been
as elaborate or commercial as our celebrations today, but we've
always had our naysayers and Christmas critics who would have us
believe that Christmases of yore were better, richer in meaning, or
simpler in tradition.

In 1904, nearly a hundred years ago, one woman wrote,
"Twenty-five years ago, Christmas was not the burden that it is
now; there was less haggling . . . less fatigue of body, less weariness

of soul; and, most of all, there was less loading up with trash." One could make the case that the real difference for the writer of those words twenty-five years earlier was that she was younger and someone else was doing the baking, shopping, decorating, and wrapping!

One year my mother gave me a bicycle for Christmas, a used bike that she told me she had gotten from the sheriff; I assumed the sheriff was a friend of hers. Only later did a friend tell me she had gotten the bicycle through a program for underprivileged kids sponsored through the sheriff's department—and for the first time I realized we were "underprivileged."

As kids, my brother and I couldn't open our presents fast enough. My mother made a big deal out of Christmas, probably giving us more than she could afford by relying on credit cards that she would spend several months paying off—just like financial advisers tell us not to do. Although I wouldn't recommend her financial excesses, I do recommend something she gave beyond the presents themselves. She gave us the gift of extravagant experiences. We never missed the Christmas parade with the lawn mower drill team wearing Santa hats or the lighting of the huge tree in the center of our town.

Contrary to the Christmas critics, Christmas is a time for extravagance. "For unto you is born this day a Savior who is Christ the Lord" went the greeting from the angel Gabriel. What an outlandish, extravagant gift! A gift of life itself. A gift that would forever change the history of the human story. The Incarnation is extravagant grace. We prepare. We shop. We again await the hearing of these familiar words we can almost recite from memory—because we are preparing a celebration of God's extravagant love.

Yes, Christmas is a time to be extravagant. But extravagance doesn't always have to come with an expensive price tag—even extravagant presents, like a long-awaited bicycle for an "underprivileged" boy.

"You come to us, O Lord.
Into our poverty comes your wealth.
Into our emptiness comes your fullness.
Into our ugliness comes your beauty.
Make us ready to open ourselves to you.
Break down the walls behind which we hide ourselves.
Quench the fear that burns in us . . .
You come, and make us rich and great and lovely.
Come, Lord, come soon."[6]

JÜRGEN MOLTMANN

Thomas Kinkade

DAY 16 | GIFTS YOU GIVE YOURSELF

Give, and it will be given to you.

LUKE 6:38

Christmas, as you know, is the
season of giving. And as the Scripture clearly tells us, giving is a
blessed thing.

At no other time of the year are we so aware of the process of
planning, shopping, wrapping, presenting. We make lists. We browse
catalogs. We wrack our brains and juggle our checkbooks, continu-
ally seeking for the gift that will inspire a satisfying "ah" when the
wrappings are pulled back.

You've probably already started. You've spent a good portion
of this pre-Christmas season thinking about what you're going
to give to those you love and those to whom you have obligations and those whose misfortune touches your heart. If you still
have a touch of the child in you, you've also spent a little time

daydreaming about what gifts you're going to receive.

But have you given any thought this Christmas season to what kind of gifts you might want to give to yourself? That's not as selfish as it sounds. And it could make the difference between a Christmas that is joyful and relaxed and meaningful and one that is stressful and tense—if you put as much care into your self-gifting as you put into the rest of your shopping.

Writer and theologian Howard Thurman, who gave me this idea in the first place, suggests two unusual but appropriate gift ideas for the self who has everything.[7]

First, he suggests you can give yourself the gift of a reconciled relationship. No doubt you can think of at least one conflict you've never really resolved this year, one misunderstanding you never had the time or energy to clear up. If you can find a way to restore harmony to that relationship, you can give yourself the gift of "peace between you and someone else."

What a great idea—giving yourself the gift of healing and peace! And Dr. Thurman has another suggestion as well. He calls it "giving a private blessing." Others have called it a "random act of kindness." The idea is quietly—secretly, if possible, and with no strings attached—to do something nice for someone else. Scrape his windshield. Bring in her paper. Write an encouraging note. By conferring upon "some unsuspecting human being a gentle grace," you give yourself the gratification of making the world a little more livable.

Those are two ideas for gifts you can give to yourself. With a little imagination you can think of many others—small investments of energy that help make your Advent season, in Dr. Thurman's words, a "good and whole and hale and happy time."

You could give yourself, for instance, the gift of honesty about what you can reasonably and joyfully accomplish during this Advent season, deliberately crossing an item or two off your must-do list. You could treat yourself to the gift of silence, even if you have to drive to the park and sit in the car with the windows up. Or you could give the gift of prayer and reflection, treating it as a privilege instead of an obligation.

Once you start thinking this way, no doubt you'll think of other possibilities for giving. But do you know, what you're really doing for yourself when you give this kind of gift? You're simply lowering your pride enough to acknowledge your need.

You *need* healed relationships . . . and the simple satisfaction of doing good . . . and peace and quiet and spiritual renewal. You *really* need Christmas in your heart and soul as well as on your calendar. And the best gift of all is that your heavenly Father knows what you need and wants to give it. By giving yourself these gifts of peace and joy and quiet, you are giving Him permission to take care of your needs. You are opening your arms to receive the eternal gift of Christmas.

Heavenly Father, Giver of all good things, I know in my heart of hearts that the best gift I can give myself at Christmas is the gift of being open to You. Please be with me in all my shopping, all my choosing, all my planning, all my crafting—my giving and receiving—and let it be all for the sake of Your Son.

DAY 17 | THE GIFT OF DELIGHT

Let your soul delight itself in abundance.

ISAIAH 55:2

Big Jim had a big garage. He had it specially built for his ever-growing collection of molded plastic, lighted Santas. Big Jim's yard was an annual "must see" when we went out driving around town to look at Christmas lights. No one could outdo Big Jim at Christmas, no one. But then, I'm not sure anyone in our small town would have even tried.

Of course, in a small town the pressure to conform runs pretty high, and most of the townspeople who entered the annual Christmas lighting contest were intent on tasteful, decorative lighting. Not Big Jim. Every year as folks from all around would clog the highway that cut through our town to view the spectacularly lit homes that lined the highway, there was Big Jim's lighted Santa display. Big Jim had his own ideas about festivity and joy and what it meant to get into the Christmas spirit.

Big Jim's notable achievement was seeing how many Santas he could put in his yard. Every year when the Santas came out, we thought he couldn't possibly add any more, but somehow he always seemed to find a way. He must have been a familiar face at the local Woolworth's or K-Mart or hardware store, because he found Santas in all shapes and sizes. His display was garish, gaudy, and overdone— he never won anything in the annual contest. But his yard was the first one kids wanted to see. His yard was the one folks talked about. And his yard was the one that I remember so many years later. Big Jim gave himself not to what would impress, but to what would delight.

When I think of Big Jim's lighted Santa menagerie, I think of Gladys Herdman in the classic children's story *The Best Christmas Pageant Ever,* and her unpolished, ragamuffin, not-quite-what-was-expected declaration, "Hey, unto us a child is born!" The Herdmans were the meanest, wildest, most unruly kids in town. No one want-ed them in their pageant, just like no one would want to live next door to a yard that looked like the result of a lighted Santa-cloning experiment run amuck. But Gladys and her siblings found delight in a story that was almost too familiar to inspire that feeling in any-one else, and they expressed that delight with all the exuberance they could muster.

I think Big Jim and Gladys Herdman had the right idea. They knew that Christmas isn't necessarily about the expected, the taste-ful, the predictable. The Christmas story is about a babe who was born to an unlikely young girl in an unlikely barn and who grew up to seek out unlikely, sometimes unruly, characters to be carriers of the good news. Big Jim and Gladys Herdman never learned restraint; their enthusiasm for proclaiming joy was over-the-top, absolute excess. If celebrating Christmas is about anything, it's about celebrating the lavish love of a God who "so loved the world that he gave his only Son."

I think Big Jim did win something after all: he won a place in our memory because he gave an entire town the gift of delight. Not all of the gifts we give and receive for Christmas are wrapped and under the tree. Some of the most meaningful gifts are the gifts of laughter, snickers, giggles, and grins; some of the most precious gifts we give are enthusiasm, delight, and the unexpected.

Dear God, open my eyes that I may see joy; open my heart that I may feel delight; open my life to the unexpected, the unlikely, the unpredictable excess of Your love, that I may be one to both give and receive delight, excess, and perhaps the unexpected. 🦌

DAY 18 | THE GIFT OF WHAT'S MISSING

May He grant you according to your heart's desire,
And fulfill all your purpose.

PSALM 20:4

I love to paint Christmas scenes—especially scenes of spacious Victorian houses all decked out for the season. I like to picture them full of families at home, bursting to the seams with delicious smells and happy laughter, while colored lights reflect on glistening snow and sleigh bells jingle.

But here's a confession: never in my lifetime have I experienced a Christmas quite like that. Neither has my wife, Nanette. Those paintings represent our Christmas dreams, not the realities of our Christmases past and present.

I never lived in a big Victorian house when I was growing up. Ours was plain and small and sort of run-down. I never experienced one of those big, warm Christmas gatherings. Our family was small—Mom, sister and brother, and me—and my working mother rarely had time for entertaining. We never had a white Christmas, either. Central California just isn't cold enough to sustain those wonderful fantasies of glistening Christmas snow.

Nanette's family Christmases also bore little resemblance to one of my paintings. Her active, adventurous parents usually made a big family trip the focus of their holidays. More often than not, her family spent Christmas in the mountains, in the desert, at the beach . . . anywhere but home. Nanette distinctly remembers a year when they decorated a cactus as their Christmas tree.

Don't misunderstand. Both of us experienced wonderful Christmases when we were children. At the same time, we felt drawn to the kind of Christmas we didn't have—and those dreams of what was missing in our Christmases have accomplished two things in our lives.

First, they have inspired paintings that seem to speak to a lot of people, and that's a joy to me.

Second, our dreams have motivated the way Nanette and I have shaped our own Christmas celebrations. We work hard to make our own home a bright, clean, welcoming place, especially during the holidays. We try to be home at Christmastime. We have even invested (with another couple) in a little mountain cabin that's almost always above the snow line in December—just right for snowmen and sleigh rides.

And what does any of this mean to you? Certainly not that you should decorate lavishly, avoid travel, or buy a cabin! My point is simply that what's missing in your life can be a great gift, the source of your greatest blessings.

It was out of what we felt was missing in our childhood Christmases that Nanette and I crafted an approach to the holidays that is deeply meaningful and satisfying to us. In other areas as well, we've found that what we lack, what we dream of, is usually a far more creative force in our lives than what we actually possess.

The places where life is unsatisfactory or incomplete or lacking—that's where we have room to grow. What we lack, what we yearn for, can fire our imaginations, motivate our actions, strengthen our faith—and those are all good gifts.

It's not automatic, of course. A lot depends on attitude.

If we let ourselves marinate in bitterness and resentment, chances are our lives will seem shabbier, less satisfactory, less hopeful by the year. But if we persist in perceiving all of life as a gift, maintaining an attitude of thankfulness even for the areas that fail to satisfy us, if we practice faith in God's goodness and keep ourselves open to the workings of the Holy Spirit, I believe we'll gradually see life changing for the better.

Maybe we'll end up with a picture-perfect white Christmas—or maybe we won't.

But we'll still be living into your dreams.

And we'll still be moving forward into joy.

Dear Father, You come to me in both my satisfaction and my emptiness, but I come to You more easily when there is an empty spot in my life. So I thank You for the gift of what's missing. I invite You to fill my dreams, shape my growth, and point me in the way of true fulfillment. ✤

DAY 19 | GREEDY!

God's grace has been revealed, and it has
made salvation possible for the whole human race.
TITUS 2:11

My brother and I were totally, completely, 100 percent boys. From BB guns to bicycles to baseballs to dirty jeans and practical jokes, we were rambunctious, rowdy boys. And for us, except in rare moments, Christmas wasn't about celebrating the birth of Christ. It wasn't about the warmth of family gatherings. No, Christmas was about how many toys we were going to get—pure and simple. We started making lists in September. We hinted. We pleaded. We were unrelenting. For us, then, Christmas was toys—the more, the better.

I think that's true for most children at Christmastime. No matter what we think or say, no matter what we try to teach our children about the real meaning of Christmas, for kids, Christmas means toys—and the more, the better.

There's a word for this, something with which we all are born, and it's called *g-r-e-e-d*. The word is harsh, unflattering, and every parent recognizes it in the endless litany of "I wants" that precede Christmas. My mother recognized it in our constant badgering.

My brother and I weren't any more or less greedy than other kids. Perhaps we have more vivid memories of what really mattered to us back then—or maybe we just keep each other honest in our storytelling. The fact is, all children are born with a great capacity for both empathy and self-absorption. All children look and reach and grab and want—unless hardship and poverty and despair have sapped their capacity for inquisitiveness, curiosity, and hope.

Is that reason to hold back the toys? Are we giving in to the greed monster when we go about fulfilling Christmas wishes?

I suppose there is a point where that could be true. There is certainly a point where we need to say no to out-of-control spending and over-the-top giving. But to hold back the toys, I think, would be to miss the whole point of giving.

"Things belong in one's growing up or else one never overcomes the need of them somehow," wrote author Phyllis Tickle. "Giftedness is a way to demonstrate love. For our children we have always seen it as a way to form a thankful, satisfied adult, to create a readiness for generosity, the early habits of appreciation, and a sense of blessedness."[8]

We learn to love by being loved. We learn to be generous by receiving generosity. We learn to give by receiving. And it's hard to embrace the "mystery" of Christmas until we've experienced the "reality" of Christmas, the tangible, the touchable—the toys.

The transformation of the "I wants" of childhood into the "I want to give you" of mature love is part of the mystery of Christmas, part of the mystery of growing in an understanding that we are, each of us, beloved sons and daughters of a gracious and merciful God. (It did happen to my brother and me, by the way, although we still have a weakness for toys.)

When we give those we love our time and our attention, when we write a "signature of love" in our homes by decorating and delighting, when we encourage the anticipation of family traditions, and even when we give them the material things that delight their hearts, we are really giving them "a sense of blessedness." We are preparing them for the time when they too can embrace the mystery of Christmas in all its fullness.

O God, children are not more greedy than I am, just more transparent, more honest. They haven't yet learned to disguise the "I wants" or rationalize the "I needs." Lord of love, Lord of my life, You know my wants and my needs in this season of giving. I lay the spoken and the unspoken desires of my heart at Your feet in this moment of quiet, and ask that You give me a knowing heart that sees with clarity the wants and needs of those I love. Let my giving be what those I love really need—let all my giving and my receiving be out of a sense of grateful blessedness. 🌿

DAY 20 | THE GIFT OF A MOMENT

I pray that…you may be strengthened in your inner
being…and that Christ may dwell in your hearts through
faith, as you are being rooted and grounded in love.

EPHESIANS 3:16–17 (NRSV)

Lead a life worthy of the calling to which you have been called, with all humili-
ty and gentleness, with patience, bearing with one another in love.

EPHESIANS 4:1–2 (NRSV)

The boy was young, no more than three or four years old. He was huddled just inside the door of the men's rest room in a large, suburban church. A crowd of mothers and children were making their way through the corridors at the other end of the building following a women's Advent Bible study. But in this rest room, near the administrative offices, the little boy had the place to himself.

The tall, middle-aged minister walked into the men's rest room and was surprised to find the little boy huddled in the corner, alone, scowling. A little puzzled, the minister hesitated, then went about his business. But the little boy was still sitting on the floor, still scowling, when the minister washed his hands.

"Are you having a little trouble?" the minister asked.

Pointing to his pants and never changing his expression, the little boy muttered, "My zipper."

The minister stepped to the door of the rest room and looked out in the hall to see if a mom was hovering close by. Not too far away stood a young mother with a stroller, an infant, and her hands full of diaper bags, bottles, and the accoutrements of young children.

"If you are waiting for a little boy, he's having a problem with his zipper," the minister said to the young mother. The mother nodded, but clearly wasn't in a position to do much. With the door slightly open, the minister turned back to the little boy and asked if he could help. The little boy stood up, grateful for the much-needed assistance. The jeans were snapped, the zipper unstuck. A minister and little boy each went their separate ways—the boy grateful, the minister relieved.

The minister didn't know how long the little boy had sat huddled in the corner of the rest room or how long before an anxious mom would have come looking—and none of that mattered. He just recognized the posture and expression of complete and utter frustration. That little boy wasn't trying to figure out what to do: he wasn't calling his mom, he wasn't tugging at the zipper. He was sitting in a corner, completely overwhelmed. He had admitted defeat.

Now, helping a frustrated little boy with a stuck zipper is a small gesture, but not one without risk in a large, suburban church. A grown man, a little boy, a rest room—and all it takes is an allegation. The minister simply could have informed the mom and been on his way. And no one is busier than a pastor during Advent. The four weeks leading up to Christmas are for clergy what the full moon is for obstetricians or Mother's Day is to florists. But this minister gave that boy the gift of time—the brief moment, the small kindness, the gentle attentiveness—when other matters were much more pressing.

In these days when the Salvation Army bell's ringing and reminds us of all we have yet to get done, our schedules, our plans, our priorities *will* be interrupted—and we will have the opportunity to give the gift of the moment. Being present to the moment matters—as a frustrated little boy in a bathroom knows.

O coming Christ, You are the Lord of little ones and little moments, and You call me to patience, kindness, and gentleness. You call me to bear with those around me in love. But, too often, before I finish my morning coffee, I am caught up in hurry and haste. Remind me this day, O gentle One, that I bear with others in love only by the grace of Your spirit within me. Help me remember a little boy with a stuck zipper when I look in the faces of grouchy retail clerks or pushy drivers in parking lots and I feel impatience and irritability rising within me. Strengthen me, O gracious God, in my inner being, that Christ may dwell in my heart. Today, let me give the gift of the moment, as I am being rooted and grounded in love. 🐛

DAY 21 | THE GIFT OF HOME

And Jesus said to him, "Foxes have holes and birds of the air have nests, but the Son of Man has nowhere to lay His head."

LUKE 9:58

Jesus answered and said to him, "If anyone loves Me, he will keep My word; and My Father will love him, and We will come to him and make Our home with him."

JOHN 14:23

I f any pervasive theme can be found in all my work, it's the theme of home. It's an important theme in my life as well. All my life I've been haunted with the idea of homemaking—creating a beautiful and safe environment where my family and I can grow together and be happy.

I know I'm not alone in this. The longing for home, the love of home, is one of the most pervasive human emotions. Something instinctive in us yearns for a place to be, a place to belong—both a physical sanctuary and a set of relationships. Most of us find great satisfaction in establishing homes and maintaining them, and being cut off from our homes can literally make us sick.

Never is this yearning for home more poignant than during the season of Advent and Christmas. "I'll Be Home for Christmas" is more than a popular song; it's also a wistful cry. The closer we draw to Christmas, the more people realize that the gift that would touch them more than any other would be the gift of being at home.

Such a sense of safe harbor, of course, is an achievement, not a given. A sense of home is cultivated by faithful and attentive nurturing. It takes work. It takes commitment. It takes a steady flow of love.

And all of us know, deep in our hearts, that even the most glowing, homelike home is still not perfect. We all have moments when we don't feel at home in our own homes, or even in our own skins.

There's a reason for that. It's because our real home just doesn't exist here on this earth. In the words of the old hymns, even the most dedicated homebodies among us are still just pilgrims and wayfarers, longing in our hearts for the place where we really belong, which is with our heavenly Father.

Jesus, too, felt this longing for His real home, perhaps more acutely than we with our spiritual shortsightedness can imagine. He knew that He was coming to this earth a stranger, that though He cherished relationships with family and disciples, He still had no place where He really belonged. It was fitting that He spent the first night of His earthly existence in a borrowed manger and the last three years of His life camping in the homes of others. The life of Jesus is one of our most touching reminders that no matter what we call home here on this earth, no matter how much love we pour into making a home for others, we'll always have that sense that we just haven't made it home yet.

And nothing could be more appropriate! As far as I can tell from the Bible, God wants us to establish homes and love each other in them. Surely, I would think, He wants us to come home for

Christmas. But He doesn't want us to harbor any illusions that any earthly home can be our final destination, even at Christmastime.

We might be home for Christmas, but we will still be journeying home—home to the heart of God.

Heavenly Father, whose heart is my original dwelling place, call me homeward once more in this Christmas season. At the same time, remind me that Your dwelling place here on earth is always in the hearts of those who love You. Teach me to make my life a place where You feel welcome and at home. 🌿

DAY 22 | WALKING IN DARKNESS

The people who walked in darkness
Have seen a great light;
Those who dwelt in the land of the shadow of death,
Upon them a light has shined.

ISAIAH 9:2

This time of year, darkness falls faster than at any other season.

Often, by the time I finish my work in my studio, the outdoor lights from our house next door have already blinked on. Night has descended, and by the time I rise to make my three-minute commute across our garden it is fully dark.

I could always flip the switch that lights the brick path leading toward the house. But the distance is not great, and I know the way. So, many evenings I choose to stumble through the shifting shadows toward our brightly decorated house and the porch-light beacon, watching for a shining glimpse of Nanette and the girls through our lighted kitchen window—and hoping I don't stub my toe.

In moments like that I get a tiny inkling of what the Scripture means about walking in darkness and seeing the light. Not that my nighttime commute is especially risky. But under other circumstances, walking in darkness can be truly daunting. And if truth be told, most of us spend a good bit of our lives stumbling along in the dark.

At times we may tread along in the twilight of confusion and discouragement, peering through the shadows for a beam of hope.

At times we find ourselves surrounded by the gloom of sin and evil—our own and the world's—fearful of death, seeking deliverance.

At times we wander through the tedium of endless nighttime waiting, watching impatiently for the change that dawn will bring.

And even in the best of times, when we think we know our way and feel ourselves walking in comfortable territory, we still walk in the dimness of our limited vision. There is so much we don't know, so much we don't understand. We don't just see through the glass darkly; we *live* behind a darkened glass, always wishing for a little more light.

What a blessing it is to hear, then, in the deepening darkness of a late December evening, the repeated Christmas assurance that there is light for all our experiences of darkness.

In our confusion and despair—surely no deeper than that of Mary and Joseph before they understood the meaning of what was happening to them—we will be given hope and purpose.

When we are surrounded by evil—as dark and demonic as Herod's command—there will be deliverance.

In our times of endless waiting—like the Hebrew people for the Messiah—we are given both the glowing lamp of His presence and the promise of dawn.

And in all our daily dimness, when we struggle to understand who we are and what we are doing, we live by the promise that all will be known. We are also given a light that shines in our present darkness—the gleaming lantern of the Lord's companionable presence, the lighted path of His Word. We are given His light to shine in us.

Best of all, we are promised that in the ultimate scheme of things, light has come out the winner. God's hope is stronger than despair. God's goodness is greater than any evil. God's dawn is brighter and longer than any night.

Light is coming. Even now, as we are stumbling in the darkness, it is already shining. The night-dark world is already turning toward the dawn, and the bright lights of home are already before our face.

One step, then another. We're almost there.

To Bethlehem, then on to Jerusalem.

To Christmas, then on to Easter.

Then, home . . . to joy.

Heavenly Father, this is indeed a season of lights shining in darkness—candles in windows, colored lights on nighttime trees, a lantern glow in a stable, a star shining high in the heavens. Help me follow the light of these images to the unquenchable light of Your real presence. ❧

Thomas
Kinkade

DAY 23 | TRUSTING THE PAINTER

For it is the God who commanded light to shine out of darkness who
has shone in our hearts to give the light of the knowledge of the
glory of God in the face of Jesus Christ.

2 CORINTHIANS 4:6

As a painter, I know a thing
or two about light.

For many years now, depicting light in all its moods has been
a goal and a passion for me. I study light. And one of the things
I have learned over the years about painting light is that I have
to paint the shadows first.

Artistically speaking, light shines in the darkness. Painted light
takes on depth and interest in contrast to surrounding darkness. And
what this means in practical terms is that I spend a good portion of
the work on any of my light-filled canvases in the process of *darkening* it.

Once the basic shapes of the paintings are blocked in, I begin
a long and painstaking process of putting down layer after layer of
tinted transparent glaze. In the process, shadows seem to fall on the

painting. Sometimes a painting eventually intended to portray sunny daylight comes to resemble a deeply overcast afternoon. A glorious dawn or sunset will look like heavy twilight. The painting grows so gloomy I almost hate for anyone to see it. Sometimes *I* hate to see it.

And yet I, the painter, know the light is coming. I can already see it in my mind, and I can hardly wait to dip my brush in gold and white and "turn on the lights" in that painting.

Now, I don't want to push this analogy too far. I don't know the mind of God, and I don't fully understand the reasons for darkness in our lives. I'm certainly not willing to state that God deliberately makes things darker for us just so we will appreciate the light! But I know that His vision for my life and for the world is for light, not darkness, and that He has already set in motion the process for bringing full light into this dark world. That's the very heart of the Christmas message.

My experience with painting light, therefore, has taught me a thing or two about living in trust when the dusk seems to deepen in my life. It's taught me that you have to trust the process. More important, you have to trust the Painter.

When I'm in the midst of the darkening process, even I get tired of the gloomy canvas staring back at me, tired of the tedious task of adding glaze after glaze. If I were living in the world of the painting, I would certainly get tired of living in twilight.

But that's where trust comes in—both for me and for my paintings. I have to trust my memory. I have to trust my experience. I have to trust the vision that inspired the painting in the first place. Most important, I have to trust in the One who holds the brush in my own life. I have to trust that when the time comes, light will shine all the brighter in the presence of the darkness.

Now, if this analogy has started to sound a bit like Chinese boxes—paintings within paintings within paintings—let's just pull back and look at the point, which is that we can depend on God's vision for the coming light.

He is dependable. He is trustworthy. And He holds the vision for this Christmas scene—a world filled with transcendent radiance.

Father of light, Creator of all things good and beautiful, I put my life in Your hands. I trust You for all the times of my life, dark and light, and I thank You especially for Your gift of light in this Christmas season.

Day 24 | A Dimly Burning Wick

A bruised reed he will not break,
and a dimly burning wick he will not quench.
ISAIAH 42:3 (NRSV)

Of all the colors of light, the warmest is the color of candlelight. When I paint light coming from the windows in my Christmas paintings, I try to capture the color of candlelight. Glowing amber. Warm. Welcoming. Nothing transforms the feeling in a room like candlelight. If Nanette did nothing else to prepare our house for Christmas, baking gingerbread and setting a room aglow with candles and greenery would be enough for me. I'm drawn to the warmth of candlelight as powerfully as summer moths are drawn to streetlights.

As evening darkness approaches, I watch in wonder as Nanette or one of our daughters lights candles in our home. Candlelight flickers, dances, and has a rhythm set to the imperceptible movement of air invisibly caressing the flame. A room may feel completely still, yet something stirs and the flame of a candle flickers.

The wick and the wax draw from each other exactly what they need to burn steadily, gently, providing light for hours. The wax slows the burning of the wick; the burning wick slowly consumes the wax. The wick without the wax becomes a fuse. The flare is immediate, intense, and short-lived—something that can't sustain itself, something used to ignite, not illuminate. A candle brings slow, steady illumination—and can't be left unattended. So too with the Holy Spirit in our lives.

"A dimly burning wick he will not quench," wrote the prophet in the book of Isaiah. In this season of winter darkness and holiday lights, a season when the call to "prepare Him room" competes with preparing everything else, I realize candles are both light and symbol to me.

We all have times in our lives when we are dimly burning wicks. We become depleted emotionally, spiritually, physically. We long for something to reignite the fire of passion, the determination of unwavering commitment. Due to grief, loss, or simply overwhelming demands on our time, we may actually dread the coming of Christmas rather than welcome the holiday season.

No matter how dimly the light of Christ burns in my life on any given day, in any given moment, or at any given time, the God of Abraham and Sarah, this gracious and merciful God we worship, is faithful. *A bruised reed he will not break, and a dimly burning wick he will not quench.* Christmas is about so much more than what we are able to prepare, create, plan, or anticipate. Christmas is about a God who comes—whether we burn dimly or not, whether our hearts feel joyful or not, whether we feel ready or not. Christmas does not depend on us.

With each match I strike, each candle I light, I remember my life is slowly, steadily illuminated by the presence of the Holy Spirit. If I attend to the matters of the Spirit, if I take a few minutes to breathe deeply, to invite the presence of God into my day, I can rest and relax in the knowledge that just as the Christ child came to a waiting manger, God comes to the waiting heart.

O God, my heart longs for Your coming. As flickering candlelight transforms a room, transform the dimly burning wick within my heart into one that is warm and welcoming. By Your grace and mercy, let me be attentive to the movement of Your Spirit as I go about my day, remembering that Christmas comes as a gift from You—not because of what I can do. 🌿

DAY 25 | THE NOW BUT NOT YET

Arise, shine; for your light has come, and the glory of the Lord has
risen upon you. For darkness shall cover the earth…but the Lord will
arise upon you, and his glory will appear over you…Your sun shall
no more go down, or your moon withdraw itself; for the Lord will be
your everlasting light, and your days of mourning shall be ended.

ISAIAH 60:1–2, 20 (NRSV)

I love snow.

It begins gently, silently. A heavy gray dominates the sky. Winter stillness hangs heavy in the air. A snowfall doesn't begin with the fury of a sudden thunderstorm. Snow falls softly. Raindrops are audible. From a barely perceptible pitter-patter to a thundering downpour, rain makes itself heard. But not snow. Snow falls silently, mysteriously transforming the world outside.

Perhaps that's why, as an artist, I've always been fascinated by snow. I love the way a whitewash of snow changes the landscape. I love the contrast of an expanse of white against the dark lines of tree branches and rooftops.

I live near the area where I grew up—a place where cold is uncommon and snow more so. As a boy, I never felt the tickling of snowflakes on my face, never knew the damp cold of mittens soaking wet from making too many snowballs. The winter scenes I paint are in stark contrast to the world outside my studio window. More often than not, when I look outside I see blue sky, brilliant sunlight, and the shade from the tall trees dappling the ground surrounding my studio.

The biblical readings from the Advent season are passages of Scripture that give us contrasting images: light and darkness, peace and strife. We live in a world where these realities coexist. Headlines give us news of conflict while we go to church to hear of peace. Relationships are filled with strife even as we worship a God of love. Is this the good news of the gospel?

When imprisoned by the Nazis during World War II, a Christian pastor and theologian named Dietrich Bonhoeffer made an interesting observation about a difference for Christians suffering the deprivation of Nazi imprisonment:

I notice repeatedly here how few people . . . can harbour conflicting emotions at the same time. When bombers come, they are all fear; when there is something nice to eat, they are all greed; when they are disappointed, they are all despair; when they are successful, they can think of nothing else. They miss the fullness of life . . . By contrast, Christianity puts us into many different dimensions of life at the same time; we make room in ourselves . . . for God and the whole world. We rejoice with those who rejoice, and weep with those who weep; we are anxious . . . about our life, but at the same time we must think about things much more important to us than life itself . . . life isn't pushed back into a single dimension, but is kept multi-dimensional.[9]

The season of Advent is about the coming of Christ, the coming of the kingdom of God. I'm told by those who know that theologians have long called this "the now, but not yet." The kingdom of God has come, but we live in a broken, sinful world. We celebrate peace, despite strife around us. We are a people of light, yet we live in a world of darkness.

So I paint scenes transformed by snow even as I work in warmth that would melt the vision taking shape on the canvas before me. I welcome the peaceful silence of snow, even as I live in a world of noise. The kingdom of God has come, but not yet in its complete fullness. *Few people . . . can harbour conflicting emotions at the same time . . . By contrast, Christianity puts us into many different dimensions of life at the same time; we make room in ourselves . . . for God and the whole world.*

Christ has come. Christ will come again.

———◦◦◦———

Stir up Your power, O Lord, and with great might come among those with whom I work, worship, play, and live. Let me walk in light, rejoicing with those who rejoice, and weeping with those who weep. Make room in my heart for the Christ child who came so long ago, and for the risen Christ who comes again and again to hearts who will receive Him. ❧

DAY 26 | NIGHT-LIGHTS

Do not fear, for I have redeemed you;
I have called you by name, you are mine . . .
Because you are precious in my sight,
and honored, and I love you.
ISAIAH 43:1, 4 (NRSV)

She has blue eyes and hair softer than spun silk. To melt her daddy's heart, she only has to look his way. The only time her hands are free of ink stains from colored markers is when she's been sick (the only time she doesn't feel like drawing); even bath time can't completely remove the evidence of an artist-at-work. She notices details others miss and is particularly fond of leaving love notes in her daddy's studio. She idolizes her big sister, but is a fearsome foe when board games come out. And this little one who is so determined to experience life to the fullest has always been afraid of the dark.

Each of our four daughters has that special something, a possession prized beyond anything else that goes with her everywhere: a special blanket, a teddy bear, a particular doll. But for this one, a night-light has special significance. An inexpensive little light that never leaves her room and with which she never plays is the key to a good night's sleep for an entire household. She's not prone to nightmares and she can't really explain why she's afraid of the dark, but knowing "there's nothing to be afraid of" doesn't dispel the fears. At bedtime, she wants a night-light to push back the darkness.

Because all kids outgrow diapers and thumb-sucking and bed-wetting, Nanette and I have no doubt that our daughter won't need a night-light on her honeymoon. But until then, while the world is new for her and monsters still go bump in the night, we make sure a night-light keeps darkness from closing in on our little girl's fears.

Each night as I tuck her in and make sure the night-light glows, I think about the difference a little light can make. The truth is, no matter how grown up we become, we all need night-lights. We all need a little bit of light to keep the darkness from closing in, because no matter what our age, fear isn't rational—fear simply is.

We fear for our children's safety. We fear for our parents' health and well-being. We fear for our own future. Some fears are big, some are little, but most fears come down to what we have no control over.

For anyone who has the privilege of parenting, comforting a frightened child changes our understanding of what it means to pray to God the Father. When one of my daughters is feeling particularly fearful and comes to me tearful and anxious, all I have to do is hold her, ask her what's wrong, then gently say her name and tell her everything is okay. I don't reassure her by telling her that nothing bad will happen. I don't try to tell her that what she's feeling fearful of is of little consequence. Again and again, children are reassured by the sound of a parent's voice, by hearing their names, by knowing they are cared for.

Those who call God "Father" are called by name. We are precious in God's sight. When we feel fearful, when we feel we are wandering in a wilderness of uncertainty, discouragement, or confusion, we are not alone. *Do not fear, for I have redeemed you; I have called you by name, you are mine.*

If night-lights weren't important, then I don't think the prophets, the psalmists, or Jesus would have spent so much time talking about light breaking into darkness. In the birth of a baby, God gave us a light that doesn't dim. The night-light in my daughter's room pushes back the darkness, as the birth of a Redeemer breaks into the darkness of a captive world. No, when my daughter is grown, I doubt she'll need her night-light; for like the rest of us who follow the light of Christ, she'll have something better.

———⟨⟩———

O God of little girls' fears and comforting night-lights, quiet the fears that distract me from living the fullness of this moment. Create in me a grateful heart, and let me know the reassurance of Your presence. In daring to call You Father, I am living the assurance that You have called me by name.

DAY 27 | HEAVENLY PEACE

I will not give sleep to my eyes or slumber to my eyelids.
PSALM 132:4

So it was, that while they were there, the days were completed for her to be delivered. And she brought forth her firstborn Son, and wrapped Him in swaddling cloths, and laid Him in a manger, because there was no room for them in the inn.
LUKE 2:6–7

Silent night, holy night, all is calm, all is bright . . .

Sound like Christmas Eve at your house?

Not ours, at least not until very late!

In a house full of small children, Christmas Eve is more likely a time of simmering excitement than of silence and calm. The day is almost here! The house has been decorated. The presents have been bought and wrapped. We've been to church. We've read the Christmas story. Now all we have left to do is climb in our beds, drift off into peaceful sleep, and wait for the morning.

But sleep—that's the problem! Who can sleep on such an exciting night?

I well remember the agony of trying to sleep on Christmas Eve when I was little. My mother despaired of our staying in bed at all. The image from "A Visit from St. Nicholas"—with not a creature stirring—was not the picture of our house on Christmas Eve. It was more the reality of two little boys popping up for drinks of water and last-minute questions and things we forgot to say, then tossing and turning in our beds, too keyed up to close our eyes.

It must have been a trial for my weary mom, who couldn't get to sleep herself until long after we did. At one point she even resorted to letting each of us open a present on Christmas Eve in hope that this little Christmas preview would take some of the pressure off our insomnia. I'm not sure it ever worked.

Today, Nanette and I relish our Christmas Eve shut-eye, but we still tend to wake a bit sleep-deprived. Our girls, though less hyper than my brother and I were, are still slow to settle on Christmas Eve. Inevitably, Nanette and I are up until the wee hours finishing something. Inevitably, we know, we'll be up at the crack of dawn. But when we do fall wearily into our bed, we find we're just as excited as the girls, and sleep is slow to come.

I really don't mind a little touch of Christmas insomnia, though. It reminds me that there was very little sleeping being done on that first Christmas Eve.

After all, a woman was having a baby—a situation hardly conducive to slumber. Perhaps a midwife was stirring around, or the innkeeper's wife was bringing swaddling clothes. Surely Joseph was pacing. Later, when the baby had arrived, there were shepherds and animals milling about, excited by what they had seen and heard. For all I know, the voices of the heavenly host were still echoing among the hills.

Surely everyone was too keyed up to sleep!

And yet surely there was peace . . . just as there is peace on these Christmas Eves when every mouse keeps stirring and sleep won't come for hours yet.

In our imaginations and in paintings, the manger scene hovers in a moment of timelessness: the mother kneeling tenderly, the father hovering protectively, the shepherds and the animals gathered closely, and the infant shining in the darkness. Amid all the noise and hubbub of that Christmas Eve night came the shining moment of wide-awake, yet perfect, peace.

I've known that peace too in the wee hours of the night before Christmas.

It's the peace of knowing that good news has come on earth.

It's the peace of knowing that all is truly well, that light has shined in the darkness, that Christmas comes whether or not we get to bed at a decent hour.

Sleep or no sleep, it's truly a heavenly peace.

Father, on this silent, holy night, grant me the gift of Your Christmas peace. Still the busyness of my thoughts, that I might be mindful that all is truly well. Grant me the grace to stand watch at the manger and then drift into trusting sleep, thanking You for the miracle of this night. 🍃

DAY 28 | CHRISTMAS CHANGES EVERYTHING

I have come as a light into the world,
that whoever believes in Me should not abide in darkness.
JOHN 12:46

Have you ever noticed how a change in light can transform the world around you?

You see it especially at this Christmas season, indoors and out.

Look around you. Ordinary houses and yards have emerged as illuminated wonderlands. Downtown light posts have become decorative sentinels. Strings of white lights wink on porches and drip from eaves, while colored lights cast multihued reflections off snowy sidewalks or rain-drenched streets. Candles and oil lamps glow in windows.

No wonder people get in their cars and drive around and gape at all these places they've seen a million times before. Everything looks completely different when the Christmas lights are out.

Indoors, too, the houses have been transformed. In our own

home, our little girls stare with wide eyes at the difference. Tiny fairy lights twinkle in the greenery on the mantel and the wreaths on the door. The tree lights cast shifting shadows on the ceiling and walls. Candles glow warm on tabletops, carving out circles of light from surrounding dimness. Firelight dances on the hearth.

All our world seems somehow warmer, more beautiful, more peaceful and joyful when the house is lit for Christmas. Dust seems to disappear. Battered, "kid-proof" upholstery looks new again. Even the inevitable clutter of four children and two adults living under one roof seems lovely instead of annoying.

To me, this entire transformation is captivating . . . and evocative. To me, it brings the reminder that the light of Christmas is supposed to change everything.

The Light of the world has conquered darkness.

Life has overcome death.

The very coming of the Christ child has transformed the universe, and we're just now in the process of trying to catch up.

This Christmas, as I gaze around me at the wonderland of Christmas lights and celebrate the coming of the Light, I find myself praying this prayer. Maybe it can be your prayer too.

Heavenly Father, Lord of light, who sent Your son at Christmas to transform the world . . . let Christmas change me, too.

Let the images, the sounds, the stories, the meanings of the season penetrate deep into my soul and make me different.

Make me a little more patient. Lot more caring.

A lot more determined to let Your light shine through me.

Let the bright reality of Christmas make me bigger—my mind more open to possibilities, my heart more creative, my dreams more compelling, my energies devoted more to others and less to self. Keep my mind and heart big and expansive like an entire gleaming heavenly host.

Let Christmas make me smaller, too—more humble, more mindful of who I am and who God is . . . but also of what God can do with something small. Make me less grandiose, less self-important. Keep my spirit small as the tiniest infant in a manger.

Most of all, let Christmas light a fire of love in me, a shining, unmistakable warmth that will be apparent to all who see me. Set me alight with both passion and compassion—for those close to me and for a world in need.

Now, in this season when the transforming light of Christmas changes everything, make me something beautiful and bright and miraculous.

You who make all things new, spark a new light in me.

Light of the world, show me how to make my own light shine.

Day 29 | Afterglow

And even now the ax is laid to the root of the trees.
MATTHEW 3:10

For thus says the Lord God, the Holy One of Israel:
"In returning and rest you shall be saved;
In quietness and confidence shall be your strength."
ISAIAH 30:15

T hey begin appearing the day after Christmas, literally overnight. For as many Christmases as I've lived, you'd think their sudden appearance would no longer come as a surprise, but it does.

I'm referring to the Christmas trees that come down as soon as Christmas Day is past. For some, December 26 is the day. For others, the tree comes down as soon as they get back in town after traveling to see family. For many, the de-decorate, reclaim-the-house day is sometime around New Year's.

Seeing discarded trees along the street, cast out, no longer valued, feels to me like showing up for a party and being told that the party's been canceled. So much takes place before Christmas that many people have lost sight of the other side of

Christmas, the afterglow, one of my favorite times of the year.

By early Christmas afternoon our family room looks like a gift wrap display exploded. The floor around the tree is strewn with wrapping paper, ribbons, boxes, and tissue. The pile is high, and the girls love the mess. Although Nanette and I do pick up enough so we can at least find the floor before the next day, that's all we do. The mess will wait. Now is the time for Christmas's afterglow.

On Christmas afternoon we take a long walk as a family, wearing or taking, of course, anything we got for Christmas—a new sweater, a bike, a hat. We breathe the December air. We listen to the chatter of our daughters. We laugh. We come home. We build a fire. We spend the evening being together, not going or doing. Sometimes we spend several days that way. We enjoy the afterglow.

Probably more so than any other month, December is a time spent *doing*. We *do* church activities, we *do* school activities, we meet work deadlines. We bake, shop, wrap, and decorate. We go to countless places to do countless things—all memorable, all enjoyable, all valuable (well, most of them)—but then comes the day after Christmas. The phone stops ringing, the hectic schedule is suspended, daily demands come to a halt—and the world of *doing* takes a grand time-out.

The tug-of-war between being and doing is as old as the Church. One only has to look in the New Testament to see a duality emerging among the disciples, from James who said, "Faith without works is dead," to John who wrote, "Abide in me." From the monastic tradition to the Salvation Army, there has long been a tension between the contemplative life and the active life. What this tug-of-war within the Church says to me is that both are important. But in our culture, *doing* comes more easily than *being*.

So in the afterglow of Christmas, we choose to resist the culture a bit. We leave our tree up. We leave the lights on. And we take a grand time-out to *be*.

It's worth the effort—and I recommend it. Savoring the afterglow of Christmas is a learned art and one worth the creative effort.

O gracious God, in these blessed days of Christmas afterglow, fill this house with faith, laughter, kindness, knowledge, patience, and godliness. Knit us together in constant affection, and turn our hearts toward each other. As a fire's hottest coals are found in the embers, may this home's afterglow be a warmth that draws others into the grace and mercy that can be found only in You. 🌿

DAY 30 | BEHOLDING HIS GLORY

And behold, an angel of the Lord stood before them,
and the glory of the Lord shone around them.

LUKE 2:9

One minute they were sitting in their ordinary spots on the hillside, surrounded by their perfectly ordinary sheep, looking up at a beautiful but perfectly ordinary starry night.

The next minute they were gaping at an angel while all their ordinary surroundings shone with the Lord's glorious presence.

Then the glory faded, and everything went back to normal—everything, that is, except the shepherds!

I can't help but wonder, though, what life was like for those shepherds in the days and weeks after the "angels had gone away from them." How did they feel after Mary and Joseph had departed and life was once more a matter of eating and sleeping and paying taxes and keeping up with sheep? What were the shepherds lives like in those post-glory days?

Probably a little bit like our lives after Christmas. For we humans, it seems, have a hard time holding on to an experience of glory.

There are times when we look around us and the world seems absolutely full of God's presence—His grandeur and splendor and goodness seem to pour from every window of our existence. Whether we feel emotional ecstasy or quiet joy or simple clarity, we know without a doubt that God is real and God is near.

But then there are times—most of the time, for many of us—when the world that meets our eyes seems just, well . . . ordinary. We do our jobs. We love our families. We know that God loves us, that Jesus came to save us. But that special, intense, gleaming presence seems like a faded memory.

This prosaic everydayness seems especially pronounced in the days after Christmas Day. We wake from visions of sugarplums to a house that needs ordering, errands that need to be run, a schedule that must be resumed. Whether you rush to get the tree out of the house before New Year's or leave it up until the last minute of Epiphany, chances are you'll still have a moment or two when you face those after-Christmas blahs.

But God's glory doesn't really fade, you know; we just have some vision problems when it comes to beholding His glory. Partly it's our human limitations. Partly it's God's "hidden" nature. But our inability to feel the presence of God has nothing to do with the reality of His presence!

What do we do when we're deep in the blahs and hungry for a glimpse of glory? We can't force the moments of spiritual clarity, but we can keep our eyes open for the transcendent moments He chooses to send us. We can fight against the tendency to grow dull and complacent and thus blind to the glory that lurks at the edges of our everyday experiences, even the most mundane.

It helps to recognize that God has a purpose for those times when His glory seems hidden from our sight. Those are the times when we learn to "walk by faith, not by sight," relying on memory and the Word and the encouragement of others, buoyed by the very presence whose glory we cannot see.

Through it all, though, we can wait in confidence. Our God can be trusted to get through to us, to give us what we need, to make us into who He wants us to be. "But we all, with unveiled face, beholding as in a mirror the glory of the Lord, are being transformed into the same image from glory to glory" (2 Cor. 3:18).

Dear Father, in these waning days of the Christmas season, grant me the grace to see things as they really are—absolutely infused with the glory of Your presence. Teach me faith and vision. Help me to be open to visions of Your glory and patient in those times when I just can't see it.

DAY 31 | WHISPER OF LOVE

A voice was heard in Ramah . . . Rachel weeping for her children.

MATTHEW 2:18

Tears come easily for little ones. When the tickling and teasing, wrestling and chasing begin in our house, sometimes gut-busting laughter gives way to tears almost instantaneously. In fact, with children there can be a brief moment when you can't tell the two apart.

Laughter and tears are as closely related as coffee and cream. And I've noticed that among adults, the ones who laugh easily, heartily, and effortlessly are usually the ones who cry the same way.

Tears weren't often a part of my growing up. My brother and I were too busy being boys. So becoming the father of little girls changed my thinking about tears. I've *now* come to realize that:

Tears can stop as quickly as they start.

Tears can say "I'm mad" as often as they say "I'm hurt."

Tears can be happy as well as sad.

Tears are as much a part of being human as sneezing, breathing, or laughing.

Tears are as true to the Christmas story as the singing of angels.

Something besides angels and glory and wise men and stars accompanied the birth of Jesus, and only Matthew tells the tale. After the wise men came looking for the child who would be king, Herod plotted to eliminate this threat to his throne. The wise men were wise, Herod was outsmarted, and Joseph, Mary, and the Christ child fled in safety. But Herod discovered he'd been tricked, and Bethlehem became a killing field for Jewish male babies two years old and younger.

Called the "Slaughter of the Innocents" by biblical scholars, this isn't a story that we read willingly, readily, or often. In fact, it's a story we'd just as soon skip over. But it's a story that makes the miracle of the season all the more compelling in these days after Christmas, when the grand time-out begins to give way to the reality of reentry.

The glory of Christmas isn't too far past before we look around and find good reasons for tears. From the headlines of the evening news to a child's tearful disappointment to the results of a biopsy, we live in a world of weeping.

"If you are past thirty-five, you surely grieve something. If nothing else, you simply grieve for the passing of time, for the swiftness with which your children are growing and changing . . . for the helplessness of knowing that tragedy can occur instantly and without warning," writes southern novelist Vicki Covington.[10]

When Matthew quoted the phrases from Jeremiah, "A voice

was heard in Ramah . . . Rachel weeping for her children," he was telling us that the Incarnation, the miracle of Emmanuel, or "God with us," is the miracle of a God who comes into the stark realism of human suffering—God is present in the very saltiness of our tears.

Pastor and teacher Dr. Gary Klingsporn wrote, "Only a Christ who comes into and shares our tears . . . only that Christ can really speak meaningfully to us today. Christ is born into whatever it is that we feel. He comes not as a predictable hero, but as a vulnerable child. From the Messiah in a manger to the King on a Cross, this is the mystery of the Incarnation—that into such a world of need, into such a world as ours, God whispered His profound love. And He whispers it yet today!"[11]

O God who entered time and eternity as a crying infant, break into my laughter and be present in my tears. I lay before You today all that burdens my heart even as I listen for the singing of angels. And I thank You for tears of memory that come with the passing of another year. 🌿

DAY 32 | TRAVEL SEASON

Jesus said to him, "I am the way, the truth, and the life. No one comes to the Father except through me."

JOHN 14:6

For a home-centered holiday, Christmas certainly involves a lot of travel.

Look at the roads this time of year. Everywhere are cars laden with suitcases and packages. Airports are crammed. A lot of people are going a lot of places. And that's appropriate, I think, because the story of the first Christmas is really one travel story after another.

Just flip through the Gospels of Matthew and Luke and see what I mean. There's the trip the newly pregnant Mary makes to visit her cousin Elizabeth. There's Mary and Joseph's uncomfortable journey from Nazareth to Bethlehem. There's the visit from the well-traveled Magi and a trip to Jerusalem to offer sacrifices. There's that long detour to Egypt.

As far as I can tell, Jesus was almost constantly on the road from the time of His conception until He was at least a few years old. His later ministry as an itinerant rabbi must have felt quite normal to Him. Traveling was the story of His life!

And traveling, of course, is the story of all our lives—whether we live out of a suitcase or hardly ever leave the house. All of us are wayfarers on the road from birth to death and beyond, and what we make of our lives depends in large part on the way we travel.

This is hardly an original observation, but I relate to it passionately because I love to travel and because I've spent a good portion of my life on the road. One summer I was actually a hobo, riding the rails. Another summer I maneuvered a borrowed Winnebago through narrow, crooked Italian streets. I've camped in Alaska and surfed in Hawaii, and even now I'm making plans to tote my portable easel to the Middle East.

Maybe this yen for travel is one reason I'm so enthusiastic about the journey called life. I love the adventure, the beauty, the unpredictability, the opportunity to grow. At the same time, I'm grateful to have the example of Jesus to follow when it comes to traveling life's highways. I'm convinced His life is the best travel guide we can have as we step out into the next year and beyond.

What can we learn from the way Jesus traveled through life? Here are just a few quick ideas that are helping me in my own journey.

For one thing, Jesus traveled light. He modeled an easy simplicity, trusting God to supply His needs. His focus was on moving forward, not staying in one place and accumulating stuff.

Jesus also traveled steadfastly. Almost from the beginning, Jesus "set His face" toward Jerusalem. He had a sense of mission about

His life and a faithful desire to keep moving toward his destiny.

More important, Jesus walked in love. Though mindful of where he was going, he was never afraid of a detour. He stopped often to heal the sick, bless the children, and answer the questions of honest seekers.

And don't tell my wife I said this, but, Jesus asked for directions. He prayed not only when He came to a crossroads, but all the time. He lived in constant communion with His Father, seeking to align Himself with God's will.

Finally, Jesus traveled joyfully. This I can't actually prove, but to me it shines from every line of the Gospels. Jesus' earthly ministry, His journey of life here on earth, carries with it an unmistakable aura of joy that shines from every step, even on the darkest roads.

And that's what we all can have in our life-journeys as well.

Jesus has already shown us the way. More important, He *is* the way.

To follow Him is to journey in joy.

Lord, You are the way, the truth, the life—my companion and my guide on the road of life. Teach me to travel simply, faithfully, lovingly, prayerfully. Teach me to travel hand in hand with You, step by joyful step.

Thomas
Kinkade

DAY 33 | A PLACE FOR GROWING

Welcome one another, therefore, just as
Christ has welcomed you, for the glory of God.
ROMANS 15:7 (NRSV)

Grow in the grace and knowledge of
our Lord and Savior Jesus Christ.
2 PETER 3:18

If you live in a household with four daughters, you're going to attend a tea party or two. I've attended a few in my time.

Like the Mad Hatter in *Alice in Wonderland,* we have quite the interesting gathering of guests at tea parties in the Kinkade "kingdom"—dolls, bears, playmates, imaginary friends. All are welcome at tea time, even daddies who have to scrunch to fit into the chairs.

With Nanette's help, the girls bake the cookies. They set the table carefully. They arrange the chairs. They pull out dresses and hats and handbags from the dress-up box and fix themselves just so. And when I hear a feminine little voice politely ask, "Daddy, would you like a cup of tea?" I think to myself, *Yep, I'll let my daughters date . . . maybe by the time they're twenty-five.*

Being a father, you see, can change a lot of things, including your thought patterns.

Without a doubt, my most memorable Christmas was the year my first daughter was born. Christmas 1988, there I was, a guy who thought of himself as a bohemian, avant-garde, outside-the-mainstream artist, who now had taken off his beret and put on a "Leave It to Beaver" cardigan, all because a beautiful baby girl had turned my world upside down. That was the first year we bought Christmas lights because, of course, I knew how much lights would delight a six-month-old baby! The tea parties would not be far behind.

Many strands of Christmas lights and countless tea parties have followed in the years since my conversion from bohemian to "Leave It to Beaver" dad. But not a year goes by that I don't think of the tremendous change children bring about in our lives.

"Our children are our most important guests, who enter into our home, ask for careful attention, stay for a while, and then leave to follow their own way . . . What parents can offer is a home, a place that is receptive but also has the safe boundaries within which their children can develop and discover what is helpful and what is harmful," wrote theologian Henri Nouwen in a spiritual classic, *Reaching Out: The Three Movements of the Spiritual Life.*[12]

Vocationally, I am an artist and Nanette is a nurse. But together our real job is that of providing a place that is receptive and within which our children can "grow in the grace and knowledge of our Lord and Savior Jesus Christ." And it is only by growing in the grace and knowledge of our Lord and Savior Jesus Christ *ourselves* that we can even begin to do the work that God sets before us.

And this word is not just for those of us who are biological parents. It's a reminder that all of us are responsible for helping the little ones of this world to grow in grace. The Christian life has always been a life lived in community. Nothing in the New Testament gives us reason to think that the life of a Christian is a life lived apart from a community of faith. Even the early monastic life was a commitment of pulling apart for a period of time in order to deepen what one brought back to the community of faith.

Growing up without a father around much of the time, I recognize the incredible gift of caring adults outside our immediate family who took an interest in my brother and me, an ongoing circle of love I see now in caring Christians who love and nurture our daughters. When Paul wrote, "Welcome one another, therefore, just as Christ has welcomed you," he was not writing to biological parents. He was writing to the community of believers. He was writing to us all.

No matter what our vocation, no matter what our age, no matter what our circumstances, we all have much to give to the little ones who will inherit our world. We all have much to bring to the tea party.

And much to receive.

From the cookies and tea of a child's table to the bread and wine of the Eucharist, we come before You, O God, sometimes eagerly, welcomely, openly; sometimes reluctantly, cautiously, with our fists clenched; sometimes awkwardly, uncomfortably. However we come, gather us into Your circle of love. Bring us to Your table, Lord, that we may grow in the grace and knowledge of our Lord and Savior Jesus Christ. 🦋

DAY 34 | THANK-YOU NOTE

Rejoice always, pray without ceasing,
in everything give thanks;
for this is the will of God in
Christ Jesus for you.

1 THESSALONIANS 5:16–18

I n our house, one of the big activities of the days following Christmas Day is the writing of thank-you notes. Nanette and I feel strongly that teaching our girls to express thanks for what they have received is an important part of teaching good manners. So we sit down together with crayons and paper (cards and pens for Nanette and me) and write simple expressions of thanks to grandmothers and aunts and uncles and friends.

It's a bit of a chore, if truth be told. It's just one more thing to do in a busy season and at a time when we'd rather be looking forward than back.

But I hope we're teaching something besides etiquette when we sit down together to write thank-you notes. I hope we're also teaching our daughters the habit of gratitude—and teaching it to ourselves as well. For I have come to believe that the right kind of gratitude is the key to joy here on this planet.

I'm not just talking about being grateful for Christmas gifts, of course, though that's part of it. I'm not just talking about being grateful for the good things in our lives, although that's part of it too.

I'm talking about a basic approach to life, a way of looking at all of our circumstances. I'm talking about learning to look at every moment of our lives as a gift to be unwrapped expectantly and used with gratitude.

And I have come to believe that if we persist in looking at all of the circumstances of life as a gift and accepting them with gratitude, we'll live happier lives. We'll feel more privileged, more gifted. More important, we'll be aligning our feelings with reality. For life, even when it's hard, really is a gift from God that calls for a thank-you. That's a message that the Bible repeatedly sets down.

It's not all that difficult to give thanks for the aspects of our lives that feel good—the job we like, the people who love and support us, good food on the table, beautiful vistas outside our front door. That's a little like giving thanks for the spectacular toys we found under the Christmas tree. Thanks come naturally, although even for these we need to remember the source of the gifts instead of just ripping off the wrapping and starting to play.

It's a little harder to give thanks for the unpleasant gifts that are "good for us"—the uncertain circumstances that teach us trust, the pain that forces us to lean on others and the Lord, the gnawing questions and doubts that spur us to dig deeper in the faith. It takes maturity to be grateful for these kind of gifts, just as it takes maturity to enjoy practical gifts such as clothing or appliances under the Christmas tree. Sometimes, depending on the gift, such maturity is something we just can't muster on our own. Sometimes we're left holding our gifts at arm's length—as my teenaged self once held the lime-green turtleneck my mother had knitted me for Christmas—knowing we should be grateful, but not quite able to muster a feeling of thanksgiving.

The good news is that the feeling of thanksgiving isn't required—just the act of thanksgiving, or sometimes even just the *willingness* to be thankful. We serve a God who takes us where we are and, if we let Him, takes us where we need to be.

Even when gratitude is a chore, the Father of lights is willing to sound the note of thank-you into our lives.

Dear heavenly Father, for the gift of life, for the gift of salvation, for the gift of Your presence, for the year just past and the year to come . . . thank You, thank You, thank You, thank You!

DAY 35 | BE SURE TO SHINE

You are the light of the world. A city that is set on a hill cannot be hidden. Nor do they light a lamp and put it under a basket, but on a lampstand, and it gives light to all who are in the house. Let your light so shine before men, that they may see your good works and glorify your Father in heaven.

MATTHEW 5:14–16

Did you know you can make a lamp out of almost anything?

It's true. I've seen it done.

With just some wires and inexpensive hardware, any object— a cowboy boot, a vase, a coffeepot, a typewriter, even a beat-up, burned-out, worthless old lamp—can become a brand-new source of shining light.

And that, I think, is good news for those of us who are called to be lights in this often-darkened world.

I don't know about you, but most of the time I feel like anything but a shining beacon of God's wonderful love. In good moments, sure, I can be dedicated and hardworking and altruistic and inspiring. But I can also be selfish and petty and egotistical and whiny. I can be a jerk. And, no offense, but so can you. So can we all.

I think that's exactly why many people end up hiding their lights under a basket. Who feels equal to the task of lighting the world?

But if a lamp can be created from the most unlikely objects, maybe that should send us a message. So should the witness of Scripture. For as far as I can tell from the Bible, God is in the age-old habit of turning the unlikeliest people into sources of light.

A spoiled, conceited young son who didn't even know when he was in mortal danger from his own brothers? That was Joseph, who saved his entire people from famine.

An Egyptian adoptee with a speech problem? That was Moses, who led God's people out of Egypt.

A shepherd boy with an ear for music? That was David, the great king and poet/composer.

The list goes on and on, all the way down to a Galilean peasant woman, her befuddled husband, and their newborn baby. And that was Jesus, "the true Light which gives light to every man who comes into the world" (John 1:9). He's been the entire focus of this beautiful season of light we're wrapping up. He's also the One who told that we are lights, no matter how we feel about our luminary possibilities.

If that's true, and we have to assume it is, how do we go about shining despite our inadequacies?

I think the key is realizing that we *are* inadequate.

We've got to realize we're not really the ones doing the shining. We're merely the lamp base, an earthen vessel that has been rewired to shine. Our job is to stay plugged in to the light and to let it flow through us, not to gleam under our own power.

On a more practical level, this is how I think it happens . . .

Our lights shine when we accept with thanks the gift of who we are—our talents, our experiences, our energies and possibilities.

Our lights shine when we then turn our focus outside of ourselves and our talents, our experiences, our energies and possibilities, when we choose to serve others.

Our lights shine when we listen to God and say yes to Him—yes to the possibility of shining, even when we're not sure how it's going to happen.

For any of it to happen, we have to stay connected to the Source of light through prayer, meditation on Scripture, and immersion in the life of the body of Christ.

It's a beautiful possibility for this bright new year. Let's stay plugged in . . . and be sure to shine.

Holy Jesus, Light of the world, I give You my life once more. As I move forward into a new year of possibilities, I ask You to shine through me into the lives of others. Despite my inadequacies, make me an example. Despite my failings, make me an instrument of Your peace and love. You have commanded me to shine . . . please help me do it. I ask it in the name of the unlikely baby who shines through this season as the one true Light.

1. Jan L. Richardson, *Sacred Journeys: A Woman's Book of Daily Prayer* (Nashville: Upper Room Books, 1996), 19.

2. John W. Vannorsdall, *Dimly Buring WIcks: Reflections on the Gospel After a Time Away* (Philadelphia: Fortress Press, 1982), 17-18.

3. Henri J. M. Nouwen, *Makin All Things New: An Invitation to the Spiritual Life* (New York: Harper & Row, 1981), 69-70, and The Way of the Heart: Desert Spirituality and Contemporary Ministry (San Fransisco: Harper & Row, 1981), 59, 52.

4. Frederick Buechner, *The Sacred Journey* (San Fransisco: Upper Room Books, 1996), 44.

5. Anne Christian Buchanan and Debra K. Klingsporn, *The Remembering Season: A Family Christmas Journal* (Nashville: Upper Room Books, 1996), 44.

6. Jürgen moltmann, *The Power of the Powerless* (San Fransisco: Harper $ Row, 1983), 19-20.

7. Adapted from "The Gift of Grace," in Howard Thurman, *The Mood of Christmas* (New York: Dodd, Mead, 1985).

8. Phyllis Tickle, *What the Heart Already Knows* (Nashville: Upper Room Books), 33.

9. Dietrich Bonhoeffer, *Letters & Papers from Prison* (New York: MacMillan Publishing Co., 1953), 311.

10. Vicki Covingtom, "Between the Garden and the Cross," *The Library of Distinctive Sermons, vol. 4* (Sisters, Oregon: Questar Publishers, 1997), 181.

11. Gary W. Kinsporn, quoted from an unpublished sermon, "The Aftermath of Christmas'" preached at First Presbyterian Church, Teague, Texas, December 30, 1984.

12. Henri J. M. Nouwen, *Reaching Out: The Three Movements of the Spiritual Life* (New York: Doubleday, 1975), 81-82.